MW01134006

LLC BEGINNER'S GUIDE

HOW TO SUCCESSFULLY START AND MAINTAIN A
LIMITED LIABILITY COMPANY EVEN IF YOU'VE GOT
ZERO EXPERIENCE (A COMPLETE UP-TO-DATE AND
EASY-TO-FOLLOW GUIDE)

WALTER GRANT

CONTENTS

INTRODUCTION

Starting a new business can be a daunting venture. It requires a certain mindset and determination. So, you would think that there are not a lot of people rolling up their sleeves to start new businesses. Yet you would be wrong. In 2021, there were approximately 21.6 million limited liability companies or LLCs in the United States and that number has been steadily growing since 2004 (Fitzpatrick, Lentz & Bubba, 2021).

An LLC is a legal entity that can give its founders liability protection while permitting them to avoid things like double taxation that other entities such as C Corporations are subject to. Hence their popularity. LLCs are so popular across the United States, in fact, that over a third of all small businesses in the country are LLCs. Of course, the different benefits that LLCs have to offer alone are not responsible for this situation. There's also the fact that LLCs are compara-tively easy to set up. I mean, if you have a good idea for a company, how hard can setting up an LLC be, seeing as millions of others have already done it?

The short answer to that question is—harder than you think. While LLCs are easier to set up compared to other types of companies, they are not exactly walks in the park. To make matters worse, it is hard to figure out exactly where you need to start if you want to launch your own LLC. Once you do find a good resource, you crack open its pages and promptly fall asleep. This is because most of the resources out there that strive to explain how LLCs work are notoriously, mind-numbingly boring. That being the case, it is not all that surprising that some people end up hiring lawyers to figure out exactly how they should go about starting their LLC. Similarly, it is not at all surprising when they come to realize that spending their funds on this wasn't exactly the best idea, especially since launching LLCs can be somewhat costly endeavors in the long run.

The thing is, though, so long as you have the right guide by your side, starting an LLC neither has to be boring nor all that difficult, at least in my experience. Growing up, I was considered a creative kid, the kind who was often defined as "off in his own world." Admittedly, I did have quite a vivid imagination and used to spend my time building, creating, and designing things. My creativity did not dwindle as I grew up. Rather, it manifested itself as a desire to build my own business one day.

Of course, this dream did not immediately come true. Once I graduated from university, I spent five years working in the corporate world before deciding to quit. Once I did, it was easy to conclude that it was time to launch my own business. I got to work immediately but to my frustration my business did not immediately take off, the way I dreamed that it would. In fact, two years in, my business still had not taken off. Far from improving, things steadily got worse until I found myself filing for bankruptcy. This wasn't enough for me to give up entirely, though. Following my bankruptcy and after taking a short break, I got back on my feet and decided to start from scratch. This time, things were different, though. Having learned from my previous mistakes, I was able to make quick progress. In just a few years, I found myself in a very different position than when I had started my first business. After all, rather than filing for bankruptcy, I was selling my second company for multiple eight figure sums.

The struggles and experiences I have gone through with both of my companies as I worked to get to this point have been revolutionary and educational, to say the least. They provided me with a perspective that a lot of people starting an LLC or considering starting one do not have but need. I know that I certainly could have used it when I was first starting out. So, why not share that perspective and everything that I have learned about forming, structuring, and managing LLCs with those that need to access that information immediately? Why not break down the entire process, step-by-step, except, this time, make it actually comprehensible and not mind-numbingly boring? Why not grant people the knowledge and insights they need to get to the point that I have and attain the success that they want without having to go through the turbulence that I had to go through?

The purpose of the book that you are currently holding in your hand is to accomplish this and more. By the time you finish reading *LLCs for Beginners,* you will have a step-by-step guide to starting your very own limited liability company. You will also know all the fundamental elements of both owning and managing LLCs, including learning the most difficult language in the world: that of taxes. Finally, you will become intimately familiar with all the pros and cons that go into starting an LLC and thus will be able to prepare yourself accordingly. By the time you are finished with this book, you will have the confidence and knowledge you need to start your very own business. That being the case, there's only one question left to answer: are you ready to begin?

1

LIMITED LIABILITY COMPANIES
IN A NUTSHELL

Most human beings want to leave some kind of mark on the world. Some achieve this through their families and children, others through great works of art, music, and literature. Still others do so by making wondrous inventions. One of the most widespread, not to mention lasting and lucrative ways of doing this is starting a company. A company that you start is not only something that can generate a great deal of wealth for you, but it is also a way of leaving a legacy to the world, something you will be remembered for.

There are several kinds of companies an individual might launch to build that kind of legacy and great wealth. From sole-proprietorships to S Corporations, general partnerships to corporations, the possibilities seem truly endless. The most popular type of business entity among all these, though, seems to be a limited liability company, otherwise known as an LLC. This type of business is so popular, in fact, that over a third of all small businesses founded in the United States are LLCs (P, 2021). But what exactly is it about limited liability companies that makes them the go-to choice for small business owners? More importantly, what is it that makes an LLC the right choice for you?

WHAT IS AN LLC, ANYWAYS?

Before we answer this question, let us first define what liability and limited liability even mean. The term "liability" means to be legally responsible and accountable for something. Limited liability, on the other hand, means the shareholders of a company are legally responsible for the debts of that company to the extent of the minimum value of the shares they possess. So, if that is the case, then what exactly is a limited liability company, or LLC?

An LLC is essentially a business structure that combines the best aspects of partnerships and corporations. As such, an LLC is able to offer its owner or owners protection from personal responsibility for any debt or liability (Kenton, 2021). This literally means that an LLC owner is not personally responsible for the liabilities and debts of his business. Hence the name "limited liability company" and the appeal. So, say that you started an LLC, got into debt with a creditor, and were unable to pay it for one reason or another. Because your business is a limited liability company, said creditor would not be able to come after your personal assets, like your house, car, or any other personal possessions (Fishman, n.d.). LLCs are a little similar to corporations in that they both offer limited liability protection to their owners and members. The key difference between the two is in how they are taxed, which we will examine in greater detail later on. For now, suffice it to say that the way LLCs are taxed tends to be a bit more advantageous than the way other corporations, like C corporations.

An LLC can pretty much take any shape or form. Someone who already has a sole proprietorship can consider incorporating and thus becoming an LLC. An LLC can be either a non-profit or a for-profit company. It can also be formed and managed by a single individual or a group of individuals. This means that LLCs can be of any size. LLCs are even allowed to own commercial and rental properties under their own names. In fact, an LLC is currently the most common entity to possess such properties (Fishman, n.d.).

One factor that makes LLCs a doubly appealing venture for prospective business owners is that they have a fairly flexible management structure, so much so that the owners themselves can determine how exactly they want to structure theirs. There's an art to structuring an LLC, though, seeing as how an LLC will be taxed will change based on how it is structured. For instance, an LLC may be taxed as a pass-through entity, where the income flows through the owner and investors. Alternatively, it may be taxed as a corporation, should its owner decide that they would prefer this form of taxation.

There are many different reasons why people form LLCs, beyond the whole legacy thing. One is that LLCs can help them generate a lot of wealth. Another is that the protection it offers to the individual means their personal assets cannot be seized in the event that their business is sued. Then there's how LLCs can help them save on taxes and even be used to buy and sell property, as well as borrow money for their businesses.

The main thing that makes LLCs incredibly popular in the business world, though, is that they are so incredibly easy to set up. The process of setting up an LLC can be broken down into six steps, which will be discussed in greater detail in coming chapters (Truic, n.d.):

- Choosing your LLC's name and registering it in your state
- Filing the articles of organization for your state
- Appointing a registered agent for your LLC
- Creating an operating agreement for your LLC
- Getting an employee identification number (EIN) from the Internal Revenue Service (IRS)
- Opening a bank account for your LLC

TYPES OF LLCS

Of course, not all LLCs are the same, as you may have gathered when you read that they could be structured in different ways. There are two main types of LLCs: single member LLCs (SMLLC) and multi-member LLCs (MMLLC). As per their names, a single member LLC only has one member, whereas a multi-member LLC is made up of at least two members (Corpnet, n.d.). Of course, this key difference leads to even more differences. For one, a single member LLC is owned and managed by the same person. A multi-member LLC has to decide if it is going to be member-managed or manager-managed.

What does that mean? A member-managed LLC is one where the LLC's partners participate in its management. These members must arrive at a majority agreement before any major decisions are made, such as whether a loan should be secured or not. Manager-managed ones, on the other hand, are managed by a specific individual or individuals within the company. Alternatively, they might be managed by a third party. Regardless, it is this manager who has the authority to make important decisions about the company.

While the primary focus of *LLCs for Beginners* is on single and multi-member LLCs, it bears noting that LLC types are not confined to these. The other types of LLCs out there are (Simon, n.d.):

- Domestic LLCs are so named because they are formed in their own home states and can therefore allow the owner to take advantage of tax benefits that are available in their state.
- Foreign LLCs are ones that are formed in states other than the owners' home states and can therefore allow the owner to take advantage of tax benefits that are available outside of their state.
- Series LLCs are made up of one limited liability company that owns smaller ones under its umbrella, which reduces the risk of financial investment for the owner.
- Low-Profit LLCs, otherwise known as L3Cs, are a kind of hybrid meant to attract both philanthropic and private investment to benefit society and generate profit, which therefore allows charities to pursue a profit while supporting their cause.
- Anonymous LLCs are structures where the owners, members, or managers are kept anonymous, thereby minimizing legal liability and protecting their data from those that would want to gain access to and use it against said owners, members, or managers.
- Professional LLCs, otherwise known as PLLCs, are formed by professionals such as doctors, accountants or lawyers, after they get a special license, which protects its owners from liabilities due to malpractice lawsuits and business debts.

Whether a company is a single-member LLC or a multi-member LLC will also impact its tax situation, seeing as the owner of the former will be treated as the company's sole proprietor, whereas the latter will be viewed as a partnership, at least where the federal tax system is concerned.

COMMON MISCONCEPTIONS

So now you understand what an LLC is, though you may still have some misconceptions regarding it. Whether you heard these from a friend, read about them online or thought of them yourself, having misconceptions can limit your ability to properly operate your business. Let's debunk some of the most common misconceptions about LLCs to provide you with a clearer understanding of this alternative company structure.

1. An LLC is a limited liability corporation and is identical to other corporations.

The true definition of an LLC is limited liability company, and while an LLC shares similarities with corporations, such as restrictions on owners' liability, it has a distinct ownership structure that puts it apart from corporations. Instead of shareholders, an LLC has members. The process of forming an LLC is also different from that of a corporation. In several states, you need to file Articles of Organization or a similar document to establish an LLC, whereas a corporation is established using Articles of Incorporation. These may sound similar and indeed they are, but the devil is in the details as they say and these small differences can create a massive difference.

2. By forming an LLC in a jurisdiction like Nevada, I can save money on taxes.

While Nevada and a few other states do not impose state income tax, you are still required to pay federal income tax on the net revenue generated by your Nevada LLC. If your LLC conducts business in a specific state, you must register your business there and fulfill the obligations, such as paying any fees or taxes required by the state, in addition to any other states that your business operates within. Having a tax presence or nexus in a state can be established through activities like owning property, conducting business, maintaining a bank account, holding meetings, or selling goods and services. The potential savings from forming an LLC in Nevada should be carefully evaluated against the costs associated with conducting business in multiple jurisdictions. So while you might be able to save taxes, it's not a given and it will depend on your specific situation. It's best to speak with a tax specialist to make sure that you are adhering to all the tax laws, they may even help you find a better way of reducing your taxes.

3. Establishing and managing an LLC is challenging and complicated.

Same people may shy away from LLC's because they are intimidated by the jargon and unique structure of the company, and believe that it will be complicated and difficult to run. The truth is creating an LLC is generally simpler compared to establishing a corporation. Unlike corporations, LLCs do not issue shares of stock or have reporting obligations to shareholders. While an LLC must register with the state, it is exempt from maintaining a board of directors or submitting detailed annual reports. The management of an LLC can be carried out by its members or through hired management, eliminating the need for a board of directors.

4. Corporations offer greater protection against liability compared to LLCs.

The term limited liability does not exclusively apply to LLCs. A limited liability company restricts the owners' responsibility to their investment in the business. Just like corporations, an LLC is a separate legal entity from its owners, and its liability is distinct from that of the owners. However, in certain cases of significant wrongdoing or fraudulent activities, a judge may hold owners personally liable. This applies to all types of businesses, including corporations.

5. An LLC is considered a taxable entity for all tax purposes.

A LLC itself is not subject to taxation. How an LLC is taxed depends on the number of members it has. A single-member

LLC is taxed as a sole proprietorship, where the income is reported on the owner's personal tax return using Schedule C. A multi-member LLC is subject to partnership taxation, where the partnership files an information return (Form 1065) and issues Schedule K-1 to each partner, reflecting their share of the earnings to be reported on their individual tax returns. A LLC can also choose to be taxed as a corporation.

IN SUMMARY

Since the process of starting a limited liability company is exactly the same, regardless of what type of LLC you are founding, which one you go for will likely depend on what you want your tax situation and management system to look like. Given that I am most familiar with single-member LLCs and their benefits, having started two in my time, the majority of this book will focus on this type. Before we can move on to all the many benefits a single-member LLC has to offer, let us quickly recap what we have learned about it so far:

- A single-member LLC is a company that only has one single owner and offers limited liability protection to that owner.
- This owner has limited liability for the obligations and debts of their LLC.

- As such, an LLC's finances are wholly separate from those of its founder.
- An LLC can be used for both investment and business purposes.
- An LLC can help protect its owner's personal assets from creditors in the event that a lawsuit is filed against it.

2

IS AN LLC RIGHT FOR YOU?

I t is great that you want to start your own company. Why wouldn't you, if you have found the next "big" idea? The question is not whether you should start a company. It is whether or not starting a limited liability company is the way to go for you. As popular as limited liability companies are, how can you know whether this type of business structure, among all the others out there, is the right one for you? To gauge whether or not you should start an LLC, you need to be aware of both its advantages and disadvantages. Only when you evaluate these things can you make an informed decision and launch your company fully prepared.

THE ADVANTAGES OF USING AN LLC

Perhaps one of the most important advantages a limited liability company has to offer is that its owner has limited liability. The limited liability protection that this business structure bequeaths to its owner means that their assets are protected in the event that creditors come knocking on their business' door. These assets can be anything from the owner's home to their car, investments, and bank accounts (Wang, 2022). So long as the company in question is an LLC, a creditor cannot lay a hand on any of these personal assets. This holds true for bankruptcy scenarios just as it holds true for situations when you accrue some kind of debt.

Another significant benefit of an LLC is that it increases a business's credibility (Dock David Treece, 2018). Starting a limited liability company basically means being recognized as a legitimate business entity by the state you live in. It means registering your LLC with your state, thereby formalizing its structure. It means sending the message to potential partners and customers that your company is both serious and professional.

Gaining this kind of credibility is something that will make dealing with financial institutions such as banks a great deal easier than it otherwise could have been. The truth is, a bank would be far more likely to extend credit to an LLC than it would to a sole proprietorship or partnership, which are individuals or partnerships that own unincorporated businesses.

As mentioned before, an LLC affords its owner a significant degree of flexibility where the management structure is concerned. An LLC can be managed by a single person, just as it can be managed by a group of owners, referred to as members, and a group of managers that are elected by the LLC's members. Members of limited liability companies can include different individuals, trusts, corporations, and even other LLCs, which is a little crazy when you think about it (Dock David Treece, 2018). Of course, single-member LLCs' management structures tend to be even more flexible than those of multi-member LLCs'.

One of the most stressful things a business entity has to deal with is taxes. Luckily, LLCs have certain tax advantages that make dealing with this perhaps daunting issue easier. LLCs are typically taxed as pass-through entities. That means that the profits and losses that come into an LLC pass directly to its owners. When tax season rolls around, the owner does not have to struggle with 50 different kinds of forms and staggering tax rates. Instead, they'll be able to file their taxes at their individual income tax rate. In other words, they'll be dealing with a much simpler process than other companies have to deal with and get to save a ton of money they other-wise would have had to spend. LLCs are sometimes even subject to certain tax deductions. One example of this is the fairly new Qualified Business Income (QBI) deduction. The

QBI deduction allows LLC owners to deduct 20% from their company's net income. This deduction comes on top of the standard business expense deductions that are applied to LLCs. So… see what I mean by saving a lot of money thanks to LLCs?

A final and tempting benefit of starting LLCs is that they tend to be very easy to set up and maintain, at least compared to other types of corporations. The process of setting up and filing for an LLC is simple and straightforward, as you will soon see. It is so straightforward, in fact, that you can finish filing all the necessary paperwork in as little as an hour.

DRAWBACKS OF USING AN LLC

Everything has its downsides, right alongside its upsides. An LLC is no exception. Starting and maintaining an LLC comes with its own unique set of drawbacks. The foremost among these drawbacks, or disadvantages, if you will, is that LLC owners have to pay self-employment taxes. Since LLC's profits flow to its owner, the IRS considers the owner of an LLC to be "self-employed". Given that, LLC owners are expected to pay self-employment taxes such as Medicare taxes and social security. The problem with this is that such taxes can add up over time. If you want to manage your money responsibly and in a way that will allow you to make more in the long run, you need to be aware of this fact before you launch your LLC.

Another drawback, or rather annoyance, that comes with starting a limited liability company is that you might have to file a form called "Doing Business As" (DBA). You will only have to file a DBA if you are living in certain states and if you want to use a name for your LLC that is different from your own. If your name is John Smith, for instance, and you have decided to found an LLC called the XYZ Company, you may have to file a DBA. To see if this is the case for you, you will need to check the requirements put forth by the state you live in.

Speaking generally, you will obviously need to comply with the laws of your state when you are founding and managing your LLC. As every state has slightly different rules about different things, you need to familiarize yourself with the state laws that may pertain to you and your LLC. It also means that you will have to register your LLC with the state and file annual reports about it. Failure to do so or to abide by any state laws will result in your having to pay certain fines. It may also result in the dissolution of your LLC, even if you weren't aware of the laws you had to obey.

While one of the great benefits of LLCs is that they usually offer their owners protection for their assets, there are sometimes exceptions. The thing is, the protection that you get from limited liability is not absolute. Certain situations, like failing to comply with state laws, for instance, can easily put your assets at risk. This is yet another reason why you should familiarize yourself with state laws. Only by doing so can you truly protect yourself, after all.

If you are going to start a limited liability company, you need to know that you will have to start keeping very detailed records. You'll need to keep a thorough record of your financial transactions and activities. This is important for both tax season and the annual reports you will be filing later on. Keeping a record of your financial transactions means keeping track of all your income and expenses—including a dinner you take a client out to. But that is not all. You will also have to keep detailed records of all your meetings as well as all the decisions that are made by your LLC. Failing to keep records of either or both of these things might well lead to various penalties and even to the dissolution of your LLC.

While starting an LLC is a fairly simple process, running one is less so. In fact, running an LLC can be a rather complex ordeal compared to running other types of companies. This is because LLCs have to follow more rules and regulations than other types of companies. That LLCs have to file their articles of organization with the state they are in or that they might have to hold annual meetings and keep detailed records of them are good examples of this. In addition to that, LLCs might have to file special tax returns and comply with state laws about employee benefits. That's a lot of things to juggle and a lot of forms to file—hence the complexity of managing LLCs.

To manage all these complexities, some LLC owners end up having to seek professional help. While this is understandable—you want to make sure you are doing everything right, after all—it can also be rather costly. Still, it is better to consult an expert when you are unsure of something than to risk getting penalized for doing something you did not know you should not be doing.

One factor that causes many people to become hesitant about starting an LLC is that forming and managing one can be a rather costly endeavor (Huston, 2021). To start, you typically have to spend more money to start an LLC than you would have to spend to start any other company. This is partly because states charge an initial formation fee when you register your limited liability company. Naturally, what that fee amounts to changes from state to state. Some states also require you to pay ongoing fees, such as franchise tax fees or the annual report. Once you do start an LLC, the complexities you have sometimes lead you to seek professional help, as we said. This only adds to the costs that LLCs bring.

You might think that starting an LLC is worth the cost, and you might even be right. But then you factor in LLCs' limited lifespan. LLCs have limited lifespans because they end up dissolving when their owners leave the business or pass away. Put simply, an LLC dies along with its owner unless specific plans exist establishing what will become of the LLC after its owner leaves. If you want to start an LLC and want it to continue on after you—in other words, if you want your LLC to be a legacy—then you might want to consider working on such a plan.

The final drawback to LLCs is that they can be difficult to raise capital for. This is because some investors, like venture capitalists, tend to be reluctant to invest in LLCs. The reason for this is that such investors have tax-exempt partners who do not want to receive any kind of business outcome given the status that they hold. Many other investors refrain from investing in LLCs because they have to spend a lot more time diligently reviewing the many documents that LLCs have to keep, and time, as they say, is money (DeGroot, 2020).

SHOULD YOUR BUSINESS BE AN LLC?

Now that you know all the pros and cons that an LLC brings with it, you are faced with a simple question: should the business you want to start be an LLC or a different kind of corporation? The answer to that question depends on you and you alone, because there is no "right" answer to give. There's only what's right for *you*. Everyone who is considering these pros and cons has to weigh them and decide for themselves. One person might decide that an LLC is the right format for them, while another might go for something else entirely. Both should take certain factors into account when deciding, though, as should you.

The first factor you need to consider when trying to decide if you want to start an LLC or not is your own financial situation. As you have seen, starting an LLC can be costly, so you need to be sure that this is a cost you can incur without straining your finances. Similarly, you need to consider what your business goals are and what kind of business structure you want. If you want a business with a simple structure that is relatively low-cost to start up, then a limited liability company is not necessarily the right business model for you. If, on the other hand, you want liability protection and a flexible management style, then an LLC might be just what you need.

What if you are not sure what you want, though? If that is the case, then you can ask yourself a series of questions to gain clarity on your wants, needs, and goals:

- What is my business goal?
- What kind of structure does my business have?
- What are my business' financial needs?
- What are the tax implications—both state and federal—that come with an LLC?
- What are the risks I'll be facing if I start an LLC?

IN SUMMARY

Once you have started answering these questions honestly, you will be able to say for certain whether an LLC is right for you, at this particular moment or not. If you have decided that an LLC is the way to go for you, then it is time to dive deeper into how to go about starting one. But before we do that in the following chapter, let us quickly summarize all the key points we have learned:

- An LLC can afford you liability protection and a flexible management style. As such, it might be a good option for you.
- However, an LLC might prove complex to run and costly overall.
- In addition to that, you might struggle to raise capital for your LLC.
- An LLC owner will usually have to pay self-employment taxes.
- If you are going to start an LLC you need to know that you will have to start keeping very detailed records.
- LLCs have limited lifespans because they end up dissolving when their owners leave the business or pass away.
- Before you decide whether or not you should start an LLC, you need to carefully consider your current financial situation, the business structure you want, and your business goals.

3

HOW TO FORM AN LLC

A journey of a thousand miles begins with a single step.

— LAO TZU

So, you have weighed all the pros and cons of starting and managing an LLC and decided that this was the right corporation type for you. Now, all that is left is for you to start your business. But how exactly are you supposed to do that? We've mentioned the six steps that go into forming a limited liability company, but what specifically do they entail? Is there anything you absolutely should know before starting this process so that you are not blindsided by anything later on? Well, you'll find out soon but first, let's take a look at the the best state for your LLC.

CHOOSING THE BEST STATE FOR YOUR LLC

You may be wondering which state to choose when forming your LLC. After all I'm sure you've heard that certain companies are based in certain states to take advantage of taxes and other laws, and you want your company to benefit in the same way. Let's look at the advantages of several states, and figure out which is the best for your new business. . After all I'm sure you've heard that certain companies are based in certain states to take advantage of taxes and other laws, and you want your company to benefit in the same way. Let's look at the advantages of several states, and figure out which is the best for your new business.

Your native state, in other words the state that you plan on actually doing business in is usually your best bet. If you choose to form your LLC in any other state instead of the one you reside in, you can still do that. The only problem is that you'll be paying taxes in any state that your LLC operates in, regardless of where its formed, so you might want to keep that in mind, nonetheless lets go over some of the most common options so that you are best informed.

Your Home State

While creating an LLC in your home state is probably your best option there are some scenarios in which you may want to register in a foreign state, such as:

If your business operates out of a different state than where you live. In this case it makes sense to register the business in the state that it operates from, keep in mind however that if you conduct business in your home state too, you'll still need to pay all relevant taxes and fees.

If your business is involved in real estate, in this case you'll want to register your business in the state where it's real estate is.

If you don't live in the US. Being a non-resident of the US will mean that the home state rule does not apply to you, so register in whichever state your company conducts business in.

Nevada

We've already covered the misconception that Nevada is the best place to form an LLC In most cases, your home state is actually the best option. Even if you reside in a state with high taxes or fees, like California or Massachusetts, the same principle applies. Let's take a closer look at Massachusetts as an example to understand why.

If you create and establish your LLC in Massachusetts, the state will recognize it as a domestic LLC since you live and operate there. On the other hand, if you choose to organize your LLC in Nevada while residing in Massachusetts, it will be considered a foreign LLC by Massachusetts. This means that your LLC was not created within the state in question.

Now, if your LLC doesn't conduct any business within Massachusetts, you generally won't encounter any issues. Perhaps you opted for Nevada as the formation state due to its absence of income taxes. However, it is likely that your business operations are still conducted in Massachusetts since that's where you reside.

Here's the challenge though, both Massachusetts, as a foreign LLC, and Nevada, as a domestic LLC, require you to register your LLC separately. This means you'll have to bear the cost of filing in two different states. You'll also have to fulfill distinct annual reporting and payment obligations for both states.

Nevada does offer advantages such as the absence of business and personal income taxes, as well as franchise taxes. However, there's a catch. These tax benefits exclusively apply to revenue generated by your LLC within Nevada. Any income earned in Massachusetts will still be subject to taxation by the state. If your business can fully operate out of Nevada, such as in the case of a fully online business, then forming an LLC there can be a great option. However, if this is not the situation, it's generally wiser to stick with your home state.

Delaware

Delaware has a reputation as one of the most business friendly states in the US. In fact, more than half of the fortune 500 companies are formed in Delaware. So what makes Delaware so inviting? Delaware's reputation as a welcoming state for companies is largely due to its business-friendly environment and well-established legal system. These include:

Corporate Law Expertise

Delaware has a long-standing reputation for its sophisticated and business-friendly corporate laws. The state has a dedicated court system, the Delaware Court of Chancery, which focuses solely on business and corporate matters. This court is renowned for its expertise and consistency in interpreting and applying corporate laws, providing certainty and predictability for companies. Its rulings have created a body of case law that gives clear guidance to businesses, fostering a stable and reliable legal framework.

Delaware General Corporation Law (DGCL)

The state's corporate law, known as the DGCL, is highly favorable to businesses. It offers flexibility in structuring and managing companies, with provisions that allow for easy transfer of shares, protection of shareholder rights, and efficient corporate governance. Delaware's laws also provide directors and officers with considerable discretion in decision-making, reducing the risk of legal challenges and increasing the ease of doing business.

Court System

Delaware's court system is renowned for its efficiency, expertise, and responsiveness. The Delaware Court of Chancery, in particular, is a specialized court focused on corporate disputes. Its judges are experienced in handling complex business matters, ensuring prompt and knowledgeable resolution of legal issues. This streamlined judicial process is particularly appealing to companies seeking swift resolution of disputes.

Privacy and Confidentiality

Delaware offers a level of privacy and confidentiality to businesses that many find appealing. The state allows the use of nominee directors and officers, which enables companies to protect the identities of their shareholders and executives. This can be a big bonus if you value privacy in your business.

Tax Advantages

Delaware offers several tax advantages for businesses. It does not impose sales tax on intangible goods or services, making it attractive for companies engaged in intellectual property, consulting, or e-commerce. Delaware has no corporate income tax on companies that do not operate within the state, known as non-resident companies.

Business-Friendly Government

Delaware's government actively supports and promotes a business-friendly environment. The state's agencies and offi-

LLC BEGINNER'S GUIDE | 39

cials work closely with companies, offering assistance, guidance, and resources for establishing and expanding operations. This collaborative approach helps companies navigate regulations, permits, and licenses more smoothly.

Delaware's Business Reputation

Over the years, Delaware has developed a strong reputation as a corporate hub. Many Fortune 500 companies have chosen to incorporate in Delaware due to the state's favorable legal and business climate.

So Delaware seems like a great choice, right? Well as with Nevada things are not that simple, Delaware has some disadvantages when it comes to forming an LLC, which include:

Higher Costs

Incorporating in Delaware can be more expensive compared to other states. Delaware charges higher initial filing fees and requires an annual franchise tax for LLCs. These costs can be burdensome, especially for smaller businesses or startups operating on a limited budget.

Out-of-State Business

If your LLC conducts most of its business operations outside of Delaware, incorporating in Delaware might not provide significant benefits. In such cases, it may be more practical and cost-effective to form the LLC in the state where your primary operations are located. This approach can save on compliance costs and eliminate the need for foreign entity registration in multiple states.

Complex Legal Requirements

Delaware's corporate laws, while business-friendly, can be complex and may involve additional administrative obligations. Compliance with Delaware's specific reporting and governance requirements might require professional assistance or extensive knowledge of Delaware corporate law. For businesses with simpler structures and operations, dealing with these complexities may be unnecessary.

Geographic Considerations

If your business primarily serves a local market or operates in a specific geographic region, incorporating in your home state can provide certain advantages. Local regulations, familiarity with state laws, and proximity to customers and suppliers can be important factors to consider when deciding where to form your LLC.

Delaware is often hailed for its robust privacy safeguards when it comes to LLC formation. While these measures offer certain advantages, it is important to note that absolute security cannot be guaranteed. For instance, even if you choose Delaware for your LLC, you will still be required to disclose your identity to banks and the IRS when setting up an account, and if you establish your LLC in Delaware but operate your business from your home state, you will need to register it there as a foreign LLC, potentially exposing the details of your business to the public.

NAMING YOUR BUSINESS

The process of forming an LLC is a fairly simple one once you have chosen your state. It's made up of six distinct steps and as previously stated, these steps are:

- Choosing your business name
- Filing the articles of organization
- Appointing a registered agent
- Creating an operating agreement
- Getting an employer identification number (EIN)
- Opening a bank account for your business

Looking at these steps, it is clear to see that the process of forming an LLC starts with a name. More specifically, it starts with your company's name. Before you can take any kind of action, you will need to choose a name for your LLC so that you can register it in your state (Haskins, 2019). Your LLC's name cannot be something that is already in use. So, if you want to name your company Maya Ziv LLC, but that name is already being used by another company, then you will have to choose something else.

How can you know if the name you have chosen for your company is already in use though? You can check whether or not this is the case by searching existing business names. To do this, you will have to go to your Secretary of State's website, where you will typically find an online entity name check. You can then use this search tool to find out whether or not the name you want is already in use. If the name you chose is already in use, then you will have to find another one. If it is not, you are free to take it and register it.

Of course, there are some additional rules you need to follow and adhere to when you are naming your LLC. These rules can be summed up as follows (AllBusiness, 2021):

- The name of your LLC has to end with the words "LLC" or "Limited Liability Company."
- The name you have chosen cannot contain the words "bank", "trustee" or "insurance company."
- The name also cannot have the words "inc.", "corp" or "incorporated" in it. Otherwise, it would run the risk of being confused for a corporation.
- It cannot be the same as the trademarked name of another entity.
- It should not be the kind of name that could limit the growth of the business in question, the way, for instance, "New Jersey Mannequins", would be geographically limiting.
- The domain name that goes with the name should be available as well. If the .com variation of that domain name is not available, you should see if other variations of it, like .net or .org, are available.

What if you know what name you want, are not ready to start your LLC yet but are worried that someone else will take the name while you wait? If that is the case, then you can always reserve the name in question. Pretty much all states allow you to do this by filing a form and paying a name reservation fee online, which might change slightly from state to state. That includes how long you can keep your reservation and what the renewal policies are (Haskins, 2022).

FILING THE FILES

Once you have registered your name, the next step is to file your articles of organization. Articles of organization, again, vary slightly from state to state, but they all have you provide certain essential information. This information can be summed up as (Haskins, 2019):

- Your LLC's name and address
- How long it will be in existence for, if it will not be perpetual
- The purpose of your LLC, which can be "engaging in lawful Activity" for flexibility's sake
- What the name and address of your registered agent are (more on that momentarily)
- The names, addresses, and contact information, meaning phone numbers and email addresses, of all

LLC members, managers, and directors, including you

You can acquire your articles of organization from your secretary of state and then file them in person or online. The good thing about these articles is that they are typically on the shorter side and are easy to understand and fill out, as you can see based on the kind of information you are expected to provide.

WHO'S YOUR AGENT?

When you are filing your articles of organization, you have to provide some basic information about your registered agent. What exactly is that? Your registered agent is the person or business that agrees to receive legal documents on behalf of your LLC. Examples of such legal documents might be subpoenas, lawsuits, official state correspondences, and annual report notices, to name but a few. Once your agent receives these things, they are obligated to pass them on to the appropriate person in your LLC. If you have a single-member LLC, that person will obviously be you. If you have a multi-member limited liability company, it may be someone else.

A registered agent may be anyone, so long as they reside in the state where you are starting your LLC. In other words, they have to have a physical address in that state, and just having a PO box will not be enough (Legal Zoom, n.d.). Of course, they also have to be over the age of 18 and available during business hours so that they can actually receive paperwork when it is delivered to them. They could be a member of your LLC, or they could be someone who is entirely separate from it.

So long as your registered agent meets these requirements, you can pick anyone you want in the state to fill this role. That being said, choosing someone with at least some kind of legal expertise is a good idea, seeing as they will be handling legal documents for you. But what happens if you choose someone to be your registered agent, only to realize that they're not a good fit for you? If you become dissatisfied with your registered agent? What if they have to move or quit? In such scenarios, you can always change who your registered agent is. Of course, you will have to pay a small fee to the state and file the necessary paperwork first.

Speaking of paying, if you really want someone with legal expertise to be your registered agent, then you can actually hire a professional one. You should know, however, that a good registered agent for hire will cost somewhere between $100-$400 (AllBusiness, 2021).

CREATING AN OPERATING AGREEMENT

Next up, you will have to create your very own operating agreement. This is not actually a requirement that is imposed in each and every state. This means that you can skip over this task in some states. So, if you are forming your own limited liability company, you should check your state's requirements and see if you have to create this document. However, creating an operating agreement even when it is not a requirement is a good idea. If you liken your LLC to a building that is under construction, you can think of your operating agreement as your blueprint. Your blueprint will show you how your building should be structured and put together, after all. Given the flexibility in management that LLCs offer, having such a roadmap can make managing one easier. This is especially true when you consider how this document covers things like ownership interests, how meetings will be held, how profits and losses will be shared, what the rights of the members are if one of them leaves the limited liability company or dies, and more.

Your operating agreement, then, is a document that covers all possibilities, contingencies, and plans you are supposed to follow should different scenarios unfold. It is your guidebook and your rule book and can help you define rights and responsibilities while minimizing any agreements that might arise between LLC members in the future.

To get a little more specific, your operating agreement should contain the following items, especially if yours is a multi-member LLC (AllBusiness, 2021):

- How much each LLC member has contributed to the LLC in terms of capital and when they are required to make those contributions
- What remedies or penalties will be applied if and when an LLC member fails to make the capital contribution they were expected to make
- How cash, profits, and losses will be distributed between LLC members
- Who will be managing the LLC
- How LLC officers will be appointed
- How voting rights will work, especially when major events like capital contributions and the sale of the business are being discussed
- What indemnification protection will be afforded to the LLC members
- What kind of restrictions will be placed on LLC unit transfers
- What procedures will be followed during meetings between LLC members
- What the procedures of dissolution will be in the event that the LLC closes

EMPLOYER IDENTIFICATION NUMBER (EIN) AND YOUR BANK ACCOUNT

The next thing you will have to do is get an employer identification number (EIN). An EIN is the identification number that the federal government—more specifically, the IRS—

assigns you for tax purposes. So, you can think of it as your LLC's social security number (SSN). You will need an EIN if your LLC has any employees or if you are planning to open up a business bank account, which you really should do.

Thankfully, getting an EIN is not all that complicated a process. Obviously, you can't get an EIN before you have registered your LLC with the state. Once you have, though, you can go to the website of the Internal Revenue Service (IRS) and apply for one online. The process of application is fairly simple, so much so that it should not take you more than 15 minutes. To get an EIN, you need to meet three requirements in total (International Revenue Service, n.d.):

- Your principal business must be located in the United States or in United States' territories.
- You must have a valid Taxpayer Identification Number such as a social security number, an Individual Taxpayer Number (ITIN) or another EIN.
- You can only apply for one, single EIN per day.

Acquiring an EIN means you are ready for the final step of the process, which is to open a bank account for your limited liability company. This is generally a good idea because it helps you keep your personal finances separate from those of your business. In light of the limited liability protection that LLCs offer, keeping your personal assets separate from your business assets in this way can only be to your advantage.

To open a bank account for your LLC, you will need to provide the bank of your choice with a copy of your articles of organization, your LLC's EIN, and your LLC's operating agreement, if you have one. If you don't have an operating agreement, you should have some other kind of document that outlines who is authorized to sign on behalf of your LLC (Wong, 2022). Once you have all the documentation you need, you will be able to meet with a banker, who will help you open your bank account.

If you have officially opened your LLC's bank account, then congratulations. This, more often than not, means that you have now formed your LLC. The key phrase there is "more often than not," because sometimes states require you to fill out some additional forms or provide some extra information to start your LLC. To see if this is the case for you, you will again have to go to your Secretary of State's website and check what their requirements for forming LLCs are. As an added step, you can and should get your business license. This way, you can make sure you are complying with all state laws, regulations, and requirements.

WHAT TO KNOW BEFORE YOU START AN LLC

Starting your LLC can be a daunting thing, even if the process to do so is very simple. This is because any new venture can be so, especially if you go into it with certain questions in your head. Given that, here are some answers to some of the unknowns you might be wondering about:

- **Where should you form your LLC?** How your LLC is taxed on the state level will vary from state to state. As such, it is important that you think carefully about where you want to form your business. During this process, consider both tax advantages and incentives that varying states have to offer and which markets you will be going into.
- **Is there actually a difference between an LLC and a sole proprietorship?** In a sole proprietorship, the owner personally owns all business assets and the business itself. This means that they are personally liable for any debts and lawsuits, which is something that can put their personal assets on the line.
- **What is a professional LLC?** In some states, some professional practices are not actually allowed to form standard LLCs. In these cases, those practices have to form what are known as professional LLCs. This rule applies to those individuals who work as doctors, architects, chiropractors, lawyers, and accountants. There is not a huge difference between professional LLCs and regular ones. The main point of differentiation is that the former has to hold a professional license to conduct business while the latter does not.
- **What is a series LLC?** A series LLC is an entity that allows assets, membership interests, and operations to be divided into series that are independent of one another. In such cases, each of these series operates

as a separate entity and has a unique name and bank account, as well as separate records. Series LLCs are often used by real estate investors who want to own multiple properties.

- **Do you need to have a business partner to start an LLC?** By now, you've probably gathered that the answer to this question will be "no", seeing as we've already discussed the existence of single-member LLCs and all. One of the great things about LLCs is that you neither need a partner nor any members to be able to form one. Owing to this, many people start their LLCs as sole proprietorships, meaning entities where they are the sole owner and operator. Doing this can be a very effective way of getting your company started, especially if you are hesitant about working with a partner.

- **Do you need to be of a certain age to be able to form an LLC?** Usually, anyone and everyone including minors can own LLCs. However, some states, such as Colorado, Illinois, Minnesota, Oregon, and Texas, prohibit this (Fishman, n.d.-a).

- **Are you allowed to have more than one member in an LLC?** As you may recall from the earlier mentions of multi-member LLCs, you are definitely allowed to have more than one member in a limited liability company. This means that your LLC can have more than one member if you want it to. An LLC can have any number of members. So, if you were to start one out with a set number of members, you can always increase it and add to it as time goes on.

- **How long does it take to form an LLC?** Considering how simple the process of forming an LLC is, it should not be surprising to hear that starting yours will not take all that long. This is another one of the benefits that LLCs offer. In most states, filing all the necessary paperwork and launching your LLC takes about a couple of business days, max. So, if you want to launch a business but do not want to wait for months, if not years for it to take off, then this kind of corporation is for you.

- **How much money does starting an LLC cost?** Another great benefit of LLCs is that starting one is not all that costly. In most states, you can launch your LLC by spending just a couple of hundred dollars. This makes LLCs a great option for those individuals who are on a tighter budget or just do not want to spend thousands of dollars to form their LLC.

- **Do you need to be a citizen of the United States to be able to form an LLC?** Actually, you do not. In fact, most of the people who start LLCs in the US are not citizens at all. Many are residents or resident aliens and foreigners as the immigration system calls them. This makes LLC a great option for people who've started businesses outside of the US but want to expand into the States without having to struggle with getting a green card or visa.

- **Do you need to have an office space to start an LLC?** Actually, a lot of people who start LLCs in the US either work from the comfort of their homes or out of places like coffee shops. So, you really do not need a physical office space to form your LLC. You can keep the extravagant sums you would have spent on renting an office space and either save it or use it for something else.

- **Are there any annual costs?** One of the downsides of limited liability companies is that you have to file annual reports when you start one. Another is that you have to pay an annual fee to keep it operational. Though this fee varies from state to state, it usually is not that much and never really exceeds $100. Some states may require you to pay bi-annual fees— meaning once every two years—rather than annual fees. Some may even ask you to pay tri-annual fees, meaning once every three years. If you want to know for certain how much and how often you need to pay, you should, yet again, check your Secretary of State's website.

- **Are there any other state laws that you need to comply with?** Yes, but you need to check the Secretary of State's website to find out what they are, seeing as they are bound to vary from state to state. It is important that you familiarize yourself with these laws as failing to abide by them can incur serious penalties. It can also lead to the dissolution of your LLC.

- **Do you need liability insurance?** While getting liability insurance is not a requirement for forming an LLC, like creating an operating agreement, doing so is a good idea. This is because such insurance can protect you from possible financial damage in the future. You might incur such damages, for instance, if your limited liability company ever gets sued or is involved in an accident. If you do not have liability insurance in cases like this, you might ultimately find yourself on the hook for thousands of dollars. So, why not cover your bases, prepare for the worse but aim for the best?

- **Can you hire employees after your LLC is up and running?** Of course you can! You can decide to hire as many employees as you would like after you have officially formed your limited liability company. If you are hiring employees, however, you should know that there are a couple of things you need to do to comply with both state and federal laws. For starters, you'll have to get workers' compensation insurance for your employees. Afterward, you will need to withhold taxes from your employees' paychecks and then pay those taxes to the government on their behalf.

- **Can one LLC own another LLC?** Actually, one LLC can indeed own another (Watts, 2021) and this can happen in a multitude of ways. A limited liability company may be shown as the designated owner of another LLC while the paperwork for that second business entity is being filed, for example. Alternatively, one LLC may end up buying another.
- **Do you have to do market research before starting your LLC?** Yes, you do have to do market research before starting your LLC, that is if you want it to be a success. To that end, you need to conduct a competitive analysis of the market you are entering. This analysis should look at factors such as market size, demand, location, prices, market saturation, business trends, and economic signs (Phelps, 2022).

IN SUMMARY

Knowing all that, the process of forming an LLC probably feels a little less daunting now. Knowledge has the power to do that. That being the case, let us quickly review what we've learned about this process, before moving on to structuring your LLC:

- LLCs are quick and easy to form.
- Your LLC's name cannot be something that is already in use.

- You need to file articles of organization with your Secretary of State's office to form your LLC.
- When you are filing your articles of organization, you have to provide some basic information about your registered agent.
- A registered agent may be anyone, so long as they reside in the state that you are starting your LLC and are over 18 years of age.
- Creating an operating agreement even when it is not a requirement is a good idea.
- Your EIN is your federal tax identification number, which you need to get.
- You should open a separate bank account for your business to keep your personal and business accounts separate.
- You do not need to spend a lot of money to start an LLC.
- You do not need to be a citizen of the United States to start an LLC.
- You can operate your LLC from the comfort of your home or even from a coffee shop.
- You need to pay an annual—or bi-annual or tri-annual—fee to keep your LLC active.
- You will need to familiarize yourself with state laws and abide by them.

4

STRUCTURING YOUR LLC

So, you have decided to start an LLC and are going to be forming it soon. But how exactly are you supposed to structure it? Are you going to form a single-member LLC, for instance, a multi-member one, or one that is a hybrid of both? What kind of LLC structure you want to adopt depends on a myriad of factors. Each structure has its own set of benefits and disadvantages. Therefore, the process of deciding your LLC structure will require taking a close look at each and seeing which one meets your needs the best, much in the same way you did when you were considering whether you should start an LLC or not.

CHOOSING YOUR STRUCTURE

When we are talking about the structure of an LLC, we are talking about how that LLC is organized and run. Before delving into the benefits and disadvantages that different structures offer, let us understand what the three types of structures are—single member, multi member, and hybrid. A single-member LLC is made up of just one member, as previously stated, whereas a multi-member one has multiple members. The hybrid structure, on the other hand, is a combination of both.

So, how do you settle on the perfect structure for your business? This will depend on a number of factors, such as your financial situation, the size and scope of your business, and your personal preferences. The simplest form that an LLC can take is a single-member LLC, as you will be its only member. So, if you want an easy, or at least easier, business to run, then this structure will be for you.

Your first step in deciding on your structure is to determine what your business's size and scope will be. This means that you need to consider things like how many employees you will have, what type of business you will be in, and whether you want to operate in multiple states or not. If you want your limited liability company to operate across many states, for instance, then you might have to go for a multi-member LLC structure. Of course, you can always start out as a single-member business and then switch to a multi-member model as you scale and expand.

Once you have decided on what your business' initial size and scope will be, you will next want to consider what your financial situation is like. This includes considering things like how much money you have set aside to start your business and whether you are comfortable going into some debt or not. This latter is especially important because raising funds for your LLC can be tricky, given some investors' reluctance to invest in them.

Finally, you will have to give greater consideration to your personal preferences as you choose your structure. To do so, you will have to ask yourself certain questions, such as:

- Do I want to be the sole owner of my business, or do I want a partner?
- Do I want to have multiple partners?
- Do I want to have employees? If so, how many?
- How large do I want my business to ultimately grow? How large or small do I want it to be when I am initially starting out?

Thinking about these factors and asking yourself these questions are important because doing so is the only way to find the structure that is just right for you. An added benefit of this process, of course, is that it will help you figure out everything you need to work on your operating agreement.

If you end up concluding that you would like to start a multi-member LLC, then there is one final decision you will have to make regarding your limited liability company: do you want your business to be manager-managed or member-managed? A manager-managed LLC is a structure where a separate manager (or managers) is chosen to handle the day-to-day operations of the business. This is a good option for those LLCs that have members that don't want to participate in management. It therefore affords members a greater degree of flexibility, reduces any possibility for confusion, and efficiently divides up the workload that needs to be done (Reuting, 2016b).

A member-managed LLC, in contrast, is a format where the LLC members, that is, the owners, participate in the management of day-to-day operations. In this structure, all members are considered managers. While you cannot prevent one specific member from participating in the decision-making process if you opt for this structure, you can limit the number of member managers that your LLC can have. You will have to specify what this cap is, though, in your operating agreement.

Whether you should opt for a member-managed model or a manager-managed one should depend on the size of your LLC. If yours is a big LLC with lots of members—say, 30 in all—a manager-managed format would be a better option for you than a member-managed one. This is because having a lot of voices involved in the day-to-day decision-making process can slow operations down quite a bit. It is also because having a member-managed format with a lot of members will cause your LLC to lose credibility if it is ever taken to court. If, on the other hand, yours is a small LLC without so many members, then opting for a member-managed model is perfectly reasonable.

As a final note, you should know that a manager does not necessarily have to be an individual person. It can also be a trust or company. Having an entity like that be your manager can have certain unique benefits. One is that it can afford you and your LLC a significant amount of privacy. After all, the fact that your manager is, say, a trust will mean you will get to list that trust's name as manager on any important paperwork, rather than your own. So, if privacy is an important matter for you, this might be a final option for you to think about.

THE ADVANTAGES OF A SINGLE-MEMBER LLC

In all honesty, the single-member LLC structure is the best option out of all of them, especially when you are first starting out. This is doubly true if you have never formed or managed an LLC before. One of the main reasons for this is that a single member LLC is the simplest and therefore most common LLC type out there. Aside from being easy to set up and manage, this structure comes with fewer compliance requirements than the others. So, you have a lot less to deal with and worry about.

One of the most appealing benefits of a single-member LLC is that, as its sole owner and member, you have complete control over the business. You can decide how it is run and make important business decisions without having to consult anyone, like a partner or board member. The autonomy that this can provide you with is certainly tempting. Of course, being the sole person making decisions about your LLC makes you the sole person responsible for the outcomes of those decisions, be they good or bad. This is the second face of this particular coin.

Moving on, another very tempting benefit of a single-member LLC is that it can help you save on taxes. The fact that an LLC is a separate, legal entity from you, its owner, means that you can deduct your business expenses from your personal expenses. You can also have your LLC taxed as an S corporation by filling out some forms at the IRS—but more on how to do that later. An S corporation is a business structure that, like LLCs, passes profits, losses, and credits directly to its owners. Taxing your LLC as an S-corp can mean you avoid having to pay self-employment taxes on your business income, which normally you are required to do (Haman, 2022).

TIPS FOR STRUCTURING YOUR LLC

Deciding on what kind of structure you want to go with before you form your LLC can be challenging. The challenge lies in figuring out which structure suits your needs and wants best, even knowing all that you know about the differences between them. Given that, here are a couple of tips that you can take advantage of while you wrestle with this question (Farmiloe, 2022):

- Ask yourself how involved you want to be. Do you want to have all of the responsibility or do you want to share that burden with others?
- Figure out your financial situation and thus what kind of funding you will need before you form your LLC.
- Ask yourself whether you are alright with being the sole person liable should something go awry or if you would rather share that liability with others.
- If you are opting for a multi-member LLC, ask yourself if you want it to be a manager-managed one or a member-managed one.
- If you are opting for a multi-member LLC, be sure to include important details like member responsibilities, duties, and the division of profits in the operating agreement to prevent issues that may occur later on.
- Consider what your business size and scope is as you are deciding on a structure for it, so that you choose the option that best fits your needs.
- If you have any questions about LLC structures or if you find that you are confused about some point or another, be sure to consult a good business attorney.

IN SUMMARY

Given all that, the fact that a single-member LLC is a very advantageous option for anyone—not just those who haven't formed an LLC before—becomes obvious. Once you have decided what the best LLC structure for you is—whether that is a single-member format or not—you can move on to actually forming your business and then managing it, which can be a complicated process if you do not know how to go about it. Before diving into how you can manage your new LLC, though, let us quickly recap what we have learned:

- A single-member LLC is made up of just a single member, as previously stated, whereas a multi-member one has multiple members.
- A single-member LLC has several advantages to offer you. These advantages are that they are simpler than other structures, have fewer compliance requirements, and give you the ability to deduct your business expenses from your personal taxes.
- On the flip side of this, though, the fact that you will have complete control over your LLC will mean you will be the only one responsible for its success or failure.
- Look at your state's requirements for starting an LLC and make note of all the advantages and disadvantages that go with different structures.

- Get professional help from a business attorney and get their take on the different structures you can go for.
- If you are starting a multi-member LLC, decide if you want it to be a member-managed one or a manager-managed one.
- A member-managed LLC, in contrast, is a format where the LLC members, that is to say, owners, participate in the management of day-to-day operations.
- A manager-managed LLC is a format where the LLC members choose a manager or managers to handle the management of day-to-day operations.

5

RUNNING YOUR LLC

You have thought long and hard about what kind of
LLC is the right one for you and landed on the
structure that suits you best. You have worked on
your operating agreement, filed your articles of organization, and basically done everything necessary to form your
LLC. However, legally forming your LLC is just the first step
to owning your own business. Now you actually have to run
it. This comes with its own set of requirements and responsibilities, such as filing annual reports, fulfilling certain
meeting requirements, and becoming very thorough at
record keeping. It even comes with certain challenges.
Failing to meet some of these requirements can cause an
array of problems for your LLC and keep it from func-
tioning to its full potential. Luckily, knowing precisely
what's expected of you and how to meet these requirements

and responsibilities in advance can help you overcome any challenges you face and solve potential problems before they arise.

TASKS INVOLVING RUNNING YOUR LLC

Managing your LLC will come with a number of responsibilities, no matter what structure you have adopted. If you want to keep your LLC operating at full capacity and grow your business in the way that you want to, you need to know what these responsibilities and tasks are going to be and have strategies in place for tackling them. Your first task in managing your LLC is to raise the funds that you *need* to manage it. This is something you will need to do immediately after you are done registering your LLC.

Begin the process of funding your LLC by evaluating your own assets (Fitzpatrick, n.d.). Depending on what your financial situation is like, you might be able to liquidate certain assets to generate funds or use them as collateral for loans. If you are able to do so, you could tap into your savings, though you should be careful about how much you are willing to invest and potentially risk. Alternatively, you might sell off some property. If you have an enquiry home, you could get a home equity loan. This is the kind of loan where you use your own home as collateral, and, of course, you can only do this if you actually own your home (Chen, 2022). This would be a rather risky move, though, because being unable to pay back your loan could mean losing your home (Fitzpatrick, n.d.). If you are understandably weary of taking this risk, you could look into borrowing from your retirement account. You should know, though, that this kind of thing typically comes with withdrawal fees, as well as tax penalties in the event that you are not able to pay them back.

If you are unable to tap into your own assets or simply do not want to take that risk, then you could think about getting an informal loan. An informal loan is money you would borrow from a friend or family member. This option can only work if you go to someone you know very well, that you trust, and who trusts you. If you are considering an informal loan, you should bear in mind that it could put a strain on your relationship with the person you are borrowing from if you become unable to pay that loan back. So, you should only reach out to the people closest to you about this matter only if you feel confident taking such a risk.

Of course, if it is a loan you want, you do not necessarily have to turn to the people in your life. You can also go to banks and credit unions and even explore government-sponsored loan and grant programs. To apply for a loan at a bank or credit union, you will need to prepare a solid business plan. This will show the lending institution that you are talking to how you expect to make a profit and grow; this will mitigate the possibility of their saying "no" to you. When talking to such institutions, you may consider using some of your assets as collateral. However, you should do this with the full knowledge that failure to pay back your institutional loan may result in you losing whatever it was you put up as collateral.

What about those government loans and grants, then? There may be federal, state, and local programs that offer such loans or special grants. Figuring out if there are any that you can take advantage of at that particular moment will require doing a bit of research. This is because such programs can target:

- Business ventures in specific industries that need growth, rejuvenation, or exploration, such as alternative energy
- Specific groups of individuals like veterans
- Certain economically disadvantaged communities or geographies that need economic rejuvenation
- Individuals seeking microloans that may start out from sums as little as $100

If all you need is short term financing, you could consider pulling out your credit card and relying on it for a constrained period of time. You might be hesitant to do so, but this is something many people have done in the past, including Larry Page and Sergey Brin, who are the founders of Google (Entrepreneur, 2008). Credit cards can provide you with immediate credit, after all, without requiring that you prepare business plans or fill out any kind of paperwork. While this can be a sound strategy when you are first starting out, it should be stressed, once again, that you should only rely on your credit card in the short term. Credit card interests can be rather high, as you know, so you would not exactly want to rack up extended credit card debt (Fitzpatrick, n.d.).

A final strategy you could try to raise funding for your LLC is to take advantage of peer-to-peer (P2P) lending sites such as Prosper and Lending Club. P2P sites, otherwise known as social lending websites, have been popping up all over the place in recent years. Their aim is to offer funding to creditworthy individuals looking to start their own businesses from various other individuals and institutional investors. The good thing about these websites is that they make applying for loans a very easy process. All you have to do is choose your P2P site and create an account. The investors will then offer you interest-based loans if they think your business idea is worth investing in.

CREATING A BUSINESS PLAN

There are many different ways you can go about securing funds for your LLC, as you have seen. A fair number of these methods require preparing a business plan. A business plan is essentially a document that defines your business' objectives and how you plan to achieve them (Hayes, 2022). Creating a business plan is a good idea, even if you do not have to do so in order to acquire the funding you need for your LLC. This is because your business plan is like a road map that you will be able to use to manage and grow your business. It can mean the difference between trying to make headway while fumbling around in the dark and trying to do so in the full light and visibility of day.

A good business plan consists of seven components:

- The executive summary
- The products and services section
- The market analysis
- The marketing strategy
- The financial planning
- The budget
- The appendix

Your executive summary should discuss your mission statement and provide information about employees, leadership, and operations. Products and services should cover what products or services your business will be offering, as well as things like how they'll be priced and manufactured. The market analysis will outline your business's competition in a detailed way and explain what niche your business will be filling in the existing marketplace. The marketing strategy, meanwhile, will be about how your LLC will attract and keep customers. The financial planning will explain how you will use the funds you have obtained or will obtain for your LLC, as well as make predictions about the future. Finally, the budget section will outline all the costs you expect to incur.

The thing about a business plan is that it is multi-purpose. You can use it to gain insights into the market you have chosen. You can use it to pick the business format that works best for you. In this regard, it can even help you write your operating agreement. You can use it to ask for funding for your LLC. If you are going to use your business plan for this latter item, including a funding request section in it is a good idea. A funding request section basically outlines what your funding requirements are (U.S. Small Business Administration, 2019). It strives to explain how much funding you will need over the next five years, as well as what that funding will be used for specifically.

When working on the funding section of your business plan, you should specify whether you want equity or debt. Additionally, you should specify what terms apply to your request and how long those terms will be valid. Finally, you should write a detailed list of everything you will use the funds you receive to accomplish. This list could include items like:

- Employee salaries if you are going to have any employees
- An accounting of the materials or equipment you will need to purchase
- The bills that you will need to pay

Once you are done with the funding request section, you might want to work on a supplementary section to it known as the financial projections portion. The financial projections section is something that can potentially convince creditors to extend credit to your business. It does this by proving that your business is and will be both stable and financially successful. If you are turning your existing business into an LLC and need funds, then including things like balance sheets, income statements, and cash flow statements in the funding projections portion will only serve to strengthen it. You can make this part even livelier and more detailed by including various graphs and charts in it.

You should conclude your business plan with a section entitled "appendix". This is where you provide supplementary documents and materials that have been requested by your potential creditors. Credit histories, resumes or curriculum vitae (CVs), reference letters, permits, licenses, patents, pictures of any products your LLC makes, and legal documents are the most common examples you could find in an appendix.

HOLDING REGULAR MEETINGS AND KEEPING THOROUGH RECORDS

Depending on what kind of LLC structure you have chosen and what your company's size is, you may be required to hold regular meetings. Seeing as you can't really hold meetings with yourself, at least not official ones, this requirement won't apply to you if you have a single-member LLC. If you have more than one member, though, regular meetings may be a part of your life for the foreseeable future. You may hold these meetings in person, via teleconference, or using apps like Zoom. In these meetings, you will typically discuss things like business progress and arrive at important decisions.

It is important that you keep thorough records of these meetings so that you can keep track of what decisions are being made and make any adjustments if and when they are necessary. Actually, it is important that you keep thorough records of everything, not just your regular meetings. This includes financial records, customer records, and employee records.

HIRING EMPLOYEES AND COMPLYING WITH TAXES

If you have opted for the multi-member LLC structure, then obviously you will have to hire employees. The same goes for when you decide to change the structure of your business from a single-member one to a multi-member one. Obviously, when you are hiring employees, you will need to comply with all the state and federal rules and regulations concerning employment. This includes getting workers' compensation insurance, which can cover employees' medical expenses, rehabilitation, and loss of wages if and when they get injured or fall ill in the course of their work (Nation Wide, 2020). This also includes paying unemployment taxes.

It is important that you find individuals who are a good fit for your company when you start hiring employees. These individuals must have the skills and experience you need to make your business a success and fulfill the responsibilities of their new positions. To accomplish this, you need to take care in how you word your job descriptions when you are looking for people to fill specific roles. These job descriptions should give a detailed overview of the responsibilities that the person filling that role will be undertaking. It should also outline things like who that person will be reporting to, what will be required of them on a daily, weekly, and monthly basis, and what their job goals will be. By making sure your job description includes all these things, you will be able to find the most qualified person for the job (My Company Works, 2017). Before hiring an employee, though, you need to make sure that they are eligible to work in the United States by filling out IRS form I-9 and checking that they have a social security number (Buehler, 2022). Once you have hired an employee, you have to report that person to your state of residence within 20 days of the hire.

Speaking of taxes, you will obviously have to comply with any and all state and federal tax laws that are applicable to you. This includes filing your annual tax returns and paying any taxes that are due when they are due. Once you do find the right employees, you will have to provide them with the training they need to perform their duties successfully and onboard them properly. Otherwise, you will end up leaving too much room for mistakes born not out of incompetence but out of ignorance. Of course, as your business grows, you will need to manage your employees carefully and ensure that their performance is up to standard. You can conduct things like performance reviews to ensure this is the case. Properly compensating your employees will also help with this, in that it will incentivize them to do their best. It will also ensure that you meet all state and federal laws concerning how employees should be paid. If you are unsure about what these laws are—for example, if you don't know what the minimum wage in your state is—you should look this information up before deciding on what wages to give for which positions.

When you are paying your employees their paycheck, you need to withhold their taxes from it, as you will be paying those directly to the state and federal governments, along with your own taxes. You will also have to give each and every employee a W-2 form to fill out at the end of each year, which is used to indicate what wages have been paid to your employees and relay that information to the IRS (TurboTax - Taxes, Income Tax, 2018).

If you are letting an employee go, that is to say terminating their employment, then you will need to follow all state and federal laws about employee termination to the letter. This includes things like compensation. If you are unsure what the rules about this are, then you can take a look at your secretary of state's website. You can also consult an attorney as needed. Consulting an attorney on matters like this and making sure that you are complying with all the labor laws that apply to your business is, generally speaking, a good idea. So is consulting an accountant, so that you can make sure you are handling your tax situation correctly as well.

INSURING YOUR LLC

One last thing you should do to keep managing your LLC to the best of your abilities is to insure it. Getting insurance is a good idea because the limited liability protection an LLC gives to your personal assets is not 100% bulletproof. It does not guarantee the protection of your assets if you have displayed negligent or criminal behavior, knowingly or not (Insureon, 2022). It also does not protect your assets if you fail to keep your business and personal assets separate by, say, opening up a separate bank account for your business.

There are several types of insurance that you can get for your LLC. The first is general liability insurance. General liability insurance will protect your assets if your customer gets injured while using your product or services, their property is damaged, or if advertising injuries like libel take place, causing you to get sued.

Other types of insurance that you could consider getting are:

- Product liability insurance
- Property insurance
- Business interruption insurance

- Vehicle insurance
- Professional liability insurance

Product liability insurance is a good idea if you are in the business of selling products. This type of insurance can protect you from lawsuits if and when a customer is injured while using your product and because of your product. In such a case, this insurance can cover the cost of your defense.

Property insurance, on the other hand, will protect your LLC in the event that your property is somehow damaged by your business activities. If a fire erupts at your office, for instance, this insurance can cover the cost of repairs.

Business interruption insurance can kick in at the same time that property insurance does. This insurance covers lost income if and when your business is interrupted by something like an accident or a natural disaster. Again, if a fire erupted in your office and caused you to pause work until the damage was fixed, business interruption insurance can make sure you do not suffer a big loss.

Vehicle insurance is a good one to get if you have to use vehicles for your business. This will protect your LLC if and when said vehicles are damaged while they are being used for business purposes. So, if your delivery truck was in an accident, then this would cover the cost of repairing or replacing it.

Workers' compensation insurance, meanwhile, can provide benefits to your employees if and when they are injured or they fall ill because of their job. Most states actually make getting this type of insurance a legal requirement for LLCs. Getting workers' compensation insurance, then, can both ensure you are abiding by legal requirements and also cover the cost of legal defense in the event that an employee sues you after suffering an accident on the job.

The final kind of insurance you may want to get is professional liability insurance, which you need if you provide professional services to others. This will protect your LLC against legal claims that may arise when a customer is dissatisfied with the services you have provided.

TIPS FOR RUNNING AN LLC

Given the unique complexities that running a business can bring, here are a couple of tips that can make this process just a little bit simpler for you (Reuting, 2016b):

- Be sure to create an operating agreement as this will help you navigate many issues in the future, such as how profits will be distributed between members and what membership interests different people are assigned.
- Make sure that all LLC members sign the operating agreement.

- Always keep very thorough records in both the digital and physical worlds. Ideally, keep your digital records on a cloud system or external hard drive so that you don't lose them. Keep your physical records in a safe and secure location that you can easily access.

- Establish a firm payment allocation system. This is the system you will use to distribute profits between members, based on their percentage of ownership. This profit distribution is alternatively known as "guaranteed payments". Guaranteed payments give LLC members the permission they need to write themselves checks, so long as the LLC in question has actual cash to dole out. Of course, specifying how this allocation system will work in your operating agreement is a sound idea.

- Keep your personal and business assets separate. To that end, consult an accountant if a member of your LLC ever secures funding or collateral for the business using their own, individual credit score. Keep a record of this so that you can keep protecting your personal assets.

- Always inform the IRS and your state about any changes to your LLC.

- Use the full name of your business, replete with the words "LLC", "L.L.C." OR "limited liability to company" when signing any document, and write down your official title at the LLC as well.

- Consider how your company might function in an international market and understand the rules and regulations of that market well before you scale your company and expand in that direction.

BUDGETING BASICS FOR LLCS

Budgeting is an important part of forming and running a successful business, and while you may hire an accountant, or even an entire department to run your finances understanding some budgeting basics will help you out in more ways than one. In fact these same basics are not limited to just LLC's and may help you in your personal life too. A well-planned budget helps you keep track of your income, expenses, and financial goals, enabling you to make informed decisions and ensure the financial stability and growth of your LLC. A full breakdown of financial management is beyond the scope of this book, so lets just go over some of the basics of budgeting below.

Setting Financial Goals

Before you start budgeting, you'll need to know your LLCs financial goals, this may tie in with your business plan, but will generally be more specific. These goals provide a clear direction and purpose for your budgeting process. Start by assessing your LLCs vision and mission and translating them into specific financial objectives. Whether it's increasing revenue, reducing costs, expanding operations, or maximizing profits, clear and measurable objectives provide a roadmap for your budgeting efforts. Consider both short-term goals (such as monthly or quarterly targets) and long-term goals (such as annual or multi-year goals) to maintain a balanced approach and ensure sustained growth.

Track and Analyze Income

To create an accurate budget, you must have a thorough understanding of your LLCs income sources. Start by tracking and recording all incoming revenue, including sales, services rendered, investments, and any other sources of income. This process will help you develop a comprehensive picture of your LLCs cash flow. Regularly analyze your income patterns to identify any seasonal fluctuations or trends that can help you make informed projections and anticipate potential challenges or opportunities.

Identify Fixed and Variable Expenses

Next, categorize your LLCs expenses into fixed and variable categories. Fixed expenses are recurring costs that remain relatively constant over time, such as rent, utilities, insurance premiums, salaries, and subscriptions. These expenses are typically essential for the day-to-day operations of your LLC. Variable expenses, on the other hand, fluctuate depending on business activity, such as inventory, marketing campaigns, employee wages, and travel expenses.

Prioritize Essential Expenses

Ensure that your budget accounts for essential expenses required for the day-to-day operations and growth of your LLC. These may include salaries, rent, utilities, taxes, loan payments, and marketing costs. Prioritizing these expenses helps you allocate funds efficiently, ensuring that critical aspects of your business are adequately funded. By focusing on essential expenses, you can maintain a strong operational foundation while carefully managing discretionary spending in other areas.

Create Realistic Forecasts

Forecasting plays a significant role in budgeting for any business. Based on historical data, market research, and industry trends, estimate your future income and expenses. While you'll want to be optimistic about your revenue projections, you should try to be realistic and conservative with your estimates. Overestimating income or underestimating expenses can lead to budget shortfalls and financial instability. Think various scenarios, such as best-case, worst-case, and most likely, to understand the potential range of outcomes and develop contingency plans accordingly.

Allocate Funds Strategically

Give priority to essential expenses, debt repayments, and investments that align with your long-term objectives. Set aside a portion of your budget for unforeseen circumstances or emergencies to ensure you have a safety net. Consider allocating funds for growth initiatives, such as research and development, marketing campaigns, expanding product lines, or entering new markets.

Monitor and Adjust Regularly

A budget is not a one-time creation; it requires regular monitoring and adjustments. Review your budget periodically, comparing actual income and expenses against your projections. Identify areas of overspending or underutilized funds and make necessary adjustments. Regularly tracking your budget empowers you to identify potential issues early on and take corrective actions. Consider implementing a system that allows you to monitor financial metrics and key performance indicators (KPIs) to assess the financial health of your LLC. By staying proactive and responsive, you can adapt to changing market conditions, capitalize on emerging opportunities, and mitigate risks effectively.

Seek Professional Advice

If budgeting feels overwhelming or you're unsure about specific financial aspects, don't hesitate to seek professional advice. Accountants or financial advisors specializing in small businesses or LLCs can provide invaluable insights and help optimize your budgeting process. They can assist in analyzing your financial statements, identifying cost-saving opportunities, developing accurate financial forecasts, and providing strategic guidance based on their expertise.

IN SUMMARY

As you can see, managing an LLC is not quite as simple as forming one. But it can be made simpler if you know what to do and how to do it. One of the most important things you need to know when managing your LLC is how to pay taxes. While this has been touched upon briefly in this chapter, let us take a closer look at how taxes work, so you can be sure you are managing every aspect of it just as you should—after we quickly recap all that we have learned, of course:

- LLCs are subject to a number of state and federal laws and knowing and complying with them is of the utmost importance.
- Complying with all laws means filing all the necessary paperwork and maintaining a registered agent in the state who can receive legal documents on behalf of your LLC.
- Begin the process of funding your LLC by evaluating your own assets.
- Create a solid business plan if you want to get a loan from a creditor.
- You need to pay your LLC's income tax.
- Not complying with all the state and federal laws your LLC is subject to may incur several penalties or lead to the dissolution of your business.

- If you want to make doubly sure that you are complying with all applicable laws, consulting an attorney and accountant is a good idea.
- One last thing you should do to keep managing your LLC to the best of your abilities is to insure it.

Let's Take a Moment to Breathe

"I don't look to jump over 7-foot bars — I look for 1-foot bars that I can step over."

— *WARREN BUFFET*

There's a lot to take in, isn't there? Let's stop for a moment and take a breather. How about a joke?

An entrepreneur explains why he started his business: "My last boss said the most encouraging sentence anyone's ever said to me – he said, 'You're fired.'"

I've always enjoyed that one – sometimes it takes a challenge to make us follow our dreams, and for many entrepreneurs, being fired from a job they don't love is the best thing that could ever happen to them.

I told you at the beginning of the book that it's my goal to break down the LLC process step by step, and create an invaluable guide that's both accessible and engaging – and the reason for that is that I want to make the LLC process as painless as I can for new business owners.

With just a few moments of your time, you can help me on my mission… and don't worry, you don't even need to leave your living room.

By leaving a review of this book on Amazon, you'll show other new business owners where they can find all the information they need to navigate the LLC landscape easily.

Simply by letting other readers know how this book has helped you and what they'll find inside, you'll point them in the direction of all the guidance they need to take the headache out of this often difficult process.

Thank you so much for your support. With the right guidance, this doesn't have to be a headache, and I'd love it if more people knew this.

Please scan the QR-code to go straight to the review page.

6

TAXES AND LLCS

Taxes are stressful and a bit intimidating at the best of times. They only get more so when you start your own business. Suddenly, you start worrying about things like tax-deductible expenses, capital gains taxes, self-employment taxes…

As complex as all this might seem, taxes do not get all that unmanageable when you form your own LLC. So long as you know what the different kinds of taxes you have to pay are, you can not only pay accordingly but also reap different tax benefits.

EVERYTHING YOU NEED TO KNOW ABOUT TAXES AND LLCS

LLCs are taxed as pass-through entities, as mentioned earlier. This means that LLCs are not taxed on their income. Instead, an LLC's owner is taxed on their share of its income. This is because both the profits and losses that an LLC makes go directly to its owners, and those owners are considered to be self-employed. This is very advantageous for LLC owners since it means they get to avoid double taxation. In other words, LLC owners find that they do not have to pay taxes on both their own individual income and their LLC's income.

Though LLCs are considered pass-through entities, you can actually have your business taxed as a corporation. That means that you can have your LLC be subject to corporate income taxes if you want to (Gellerman, 2021). After all, corporate income taxes tend to be lower than personal tax rates. This is a good option to keep in mind when your LLC starts earning a lot of income. One type of corporation that you can have your LLC taxed as is an S corporation. Doing so would give you the ability to deduct certain business expenses on your corporate tax return. So, again, this might be an option to consider if you typically have a lot of business expenses or hefty ones.

Another kind of corporation that you can have your LLC taxed as is a C corporation. A C corporation is a legal entity, like an S corporation. The difference between a C corporation and an S corp is that in C corporations, business owners and shareholders are taxed separately from the business entity in question (Kagan, 2019). Given that, you might want to consider having your LLC taxed as a C corporation if you have investors who want the business to be treated as a separate entity for tax purposes.

Regardless of how your LLC is taxed, though, you yourself will always have to pay self-employment taxes if you are the owner of your LLC. The same goes for any partners you may have. This is, again, because the profits your LLC obtains will go directly to you and your partners, if you have them. Self-employment taxes, as you know, cover social security and Medicare.

There is also the main federal tax to pay. The way you pay your federal taxes changes depending on whether you have a single-member LLC or a multi-member one. If you have a single-member LLC, you will be filing your taxes as a sole proprietor by preparing a profit-loss statement on IRS Schedule C, then filing Form 1040. If you have a multi-member entity, on the other hand, you will have to file as a "partnership" rather than a sole-proprietor. This means you follow the instructions given in IRS Form 1065 and prepare a Schedule K-1 (a profit and loss statement) for each member. In both cases, though, you file your taxes using Form 8832 after completing these steps (Broussard, 2022).

In addition to federal taxes, there will be certain state taxes you may be subject to, as you might have guessed. What kinds of state taxes you are subject to will depend on which state you live in. For example, some states have a corporate income tax that they require you to pay. Others levy taxes such as the franchise tax, which is a tax you pay for your LLC's right to exist and do business in a particular state (Cornell Law School, n.d.). Still others might impose a gross receipts tax, which is applied to the total gross revenues your LLC will make (Tax Foundation, n.d.). Obviously, if you want to know exactly which state taxes you will be expected to pay, you will need to check the website of your state's tax authority. That way you will not be caught off guard by any.

Unfortunately, there is one additional kind of tax you may have to pay, and that is local tax (Gellerman, 2021). Whether or not you are subject to any local taxes depends on which city and county you are in. For example, a lot of cities and counties require that you pay something called the business license tax. This is a tax that requires you to make a contribution to the municipality you are in (Municipal Association of South Carolina, n.d.). Other cities or counties sometimes require that you pay something called a gross receipts tax. This is a tax that is paid on the gross sales of a business (Murray, 2022). Local taxes like these are typically calculated based on how much revenue your LLC generates with its business activities.

Now, there are a couple of things you have to do, on top of paying your federal, state, and local taxes, after you have launched your LLC. For instance, if you expect to owe at least $1,000 in taxes, you have to pay something called "estimated taxes." Estimated taxes are generally paid a couple of times throughout the year. They are calculated based on the amount of money you will be owed for the year (Gellerman, 2021). Hence the "estimated" portion of the name. These taxes are paid four times a year, meaning quarterly, and failure to pay them can cause you to get fined. It can also incur certain interest charges.

As for you reporting your income, you need to report your share of your LLC's income on your personal tax returns. This is just as true for state taxes as it is for federal ones. On top of that, you should know that LLCs are expected to file annual tax returns every April 15th. To do this, you will need to fill out and file Form 1040. You may also have to file a state tax return, and you should check your state's tax website to see if this is the case for you.

Considering the different taxes you may have to pay and how confusing the process of paying them can sometimes appear to be, consulting an accountant might be a good idea when trying to figure out your tax situation. This is especially true for those individuals who've never founded an LLC or any other kind of company before.

HOW TO MAKE TAXES WORK FOR YOU

Starting your very own LLC is actually something that comes with unique tax benefits. One such benefit is that, unlike other business entities like corporations, your LLC will not have to pay any taxes until and unless it starts making a profit. Another is that by having an LLC, you avoid double taxation, as mentioned before. Still another is that you may become eligible for a small business owner tax deduction (Broussard, 2022). As per the name, this deduction is only available for small businesses and is known as the Qualified Business Income Deduction (QBI).

Basically, QBI gives you an extra deduction for your normal business expenses on your income tax returns. This is in addition to the normal business expenses you can deduct from your taxable income. Examples of such expenses include the cost of office supplies, office rent, employee salaries, and travel expenses, if they are applicable.

The good thing about tax deductions like this is that they help reduce the amount of taxes that your LLC is owed. This amount might be reduced further if you claim a tax deduction on capital expenditures for express business use. So, if your business has assets like machinery, vehicles, and buildings, you can deduct these costs as well (Murray, 2021). Add to that the freedom you have to decide on how exactly you want to be taxed—whether as a sole proprietorship, S corporation, C corporation, or multi-owner partnership—and it is clear to see just how much of a headache LLCs can save you from when tax season hits.

If you want to have your LLC be taxed as a C corporation rather than accept the default tax classification that is given to your business, then you will need to file Form 8832, Entity Classification Election, with the IRS (Murray, 2022b). The first part of this form will help you determine whether or not your business is eligible for the change you want. Hint: since your business is an LLC, it most likely is eligible. The second part of the form will have you select what type of entity your current business is. Then it will let you choose what you want it to be classified as. Once you have filled out both parts of the form, all you will need to do is sign it and wait.

If, on the other hand, you would like for your LLC to be classified as an S corporation, you will have to file Form 2553, Election by a Small Business Corporation, with the IRS. This form works much the same way the previous one does. The thing about Form 2553, though, is that you need to file it no more than two months and 15 days after the tax year has begun. To time this effectively, you will need to designate an election effective date, meaning a date when your change goes into effect.

TIPS FOR MANAGING TAX SEASON AS AN LLC OWNER

Your first tax season as an LLC owner may be a rather stressful one, or at least more stressful than usual. Given that, here are a couple of handy tips you could make use of when you have to tackle the taxes (Prakash, 2020):

- Find a good accountant that you trust and hire them if you can. If you can't, then at least consult them on points that confuse you.
- Take advantage of any and all tax deductions and tax credits that you are eligible for. To that end, research your state's tax regulations well.
- Review your tax deadlines ahead of tax season and write down relevant due dates in either your physical calendar or your electronic calendar. If you enter this information into your electronic calendar, make sure you set alarms for yourself.
- Make sure you understand all the federal, state, and local tax regulations that apply to you.
- Since the IRS allows LLCs to deduct or write off any supply or equipment purchases that you make while running your business, so long as they are used within the United States, as opposed to in foreign countries. If you have purchased any such supplies or equipment, then, you should hold onto the receipts for them until tax season rolls around.

- If you have been traveling for business purposes, the money you have spent on travel will be tax deductible. Any income you have spent on things like trade conventions or conferences will similarly be tax deductible.

- Hiring motivational speakers, holding seminars and training sessions for your employees and other similar activities count as tax-deductible business expenses. So do subscriptions to any trade publications, magazines or newspapers that you have made for business-related reasons.

- Any fees you may have paid to acquire business licenses and permits are tax deductible, along with any amount of money your LLC has paid to a professional association of some kind. Examples of such things might be resale licenses, sales permits, and any other kind of similar, legal documentation.

- Familiarize yourself with tax-related jargon, such as revenue, net sales, and gross profit. This will help you to better understand your tax return, especially if you are doing it without turning to an accountant.

- Make sure you always keep very accurate records. This means holding onto everything from bank statements to invoices and keeping them in a well-organized file.

- Know that you can make tax deductions by contributing to your retirement account. Deduction limits can vary, though, so do your research about

this in advance and adjust your contributions
accordingly

IN SUMMARY

While LLCs come with certain benefits—like the tax advantages we were just talking about—they also come with certain risks as well. Some of these risks are specific to single-member LLCs. If you are considering starting a single-member LLC for yourself, then you need to do so in full awareness of the risks. Before we discuss those risks at length, though, let us quickly go over all the benefits we just discussed:

- LLCs are taxed as pass-through entities, meaning that the owners of the LLC pay taxes on the LLC's income on their personal tax returns.
- LLCs can choose to be taxed as C corporations and S corporations, and both of these things come with their own tax implications.
- LLC can deduct business expenses which can reduce how much they owe in taxes.
- LLCs must pay self-employment taxes if they have any members who are considered self-employed.
- LLCs pay both state and federal taxes, depending on which state they are in.
- All LLCs must file their annual tax return (Form 1040) and state tax returns (if applicable). While they are at it, they must pay estimated taxes, assuming they anticipate having to pay at least $1,000 in taxes in a single tax year.

7

THE RISKS OF
SINGLE-MEMBER LLCS

W hile a single-member LLC is the simplest and most flexible type of LLC you could form, it does have certain risks, just as any business venture does. These risks range from the difficulty of raising capital to the fact that single-member LLC owners are personally liable for all the obligations and debts of their business. It is incredibly important that you be aware of these risks, so you can plan accordingly and know how to mitigate them. It is equally important to know which alternative business model you can use as you work to launch your company.

WHAT RISKS, SPECIFICALLY?

One of the biggest drawbacks of single-member LLCs is that their owner bears full responsibility for things that may go wrong. A single-member LLC does not involve any other members by its very definition. The owner is the sole individual making decisions. That means that the onus of a wrong decision is on them and them alone. This can prove problematic under several circumstances. If, for instance, an LLC owner has incurred business debts and if they haven't kept their business and personal assets separate, this could put their personal assets at risk. The limited liability protection that LLCs afford their owners might not really do much in this case. Neither would it do much of anything if the case were to go to court and the court were to decide that the owner of a single-member LLC was personally liable for those debts (UpCounsel, n.d.).

At present, only three states in the US afford single-member LLCs the same kind of protection that is afforded to traditional, multi-member LLCs. On top of that, some states go as far as to deny protection to the owners of SMLCCs. That being the case, it is important that you look up the limited liability laws of your state as they pertain to single-member LLCs if you are considering starting your own.

Another disadvantage that comes with single-member LLCs is that their owners are subject to self-employment taxes.

While the reasons for this make sense, it does not change how great an expense self-employment taxes can sometimes amount to. This—compounded with how hard it may be for LLCs to raise capital given certain investors' reluctance to do so—can put a certain degree of financial strain on an LLC owner.

ALTERNATIVES TO THE LLC ROUTE

The most appealing features of LLCs are their flexibility and simplicity, as we have said. But they can come with some unique quirks. As such, thinking about starting a different kind of company than an LLC is very understandable. Luckily, there are alternative corporation models you could consider adopting that have similar advantages to LLCs without the disadvantages.

The first of these possible models are sole proprietorships and partnerships. A sole proprietorship can be defined as a business that is owned by a single individual (Chaves, n.d.). A boutique or a corner bookshop, for instance, might be examples of sole proprietorships. So might a construction contractor. The defining feature of sole proprietorships is that they allow their owners to reap all the financial profits that their business offers up. They also get to pay lower taxes as their income is considered to be their personal earnings. On the flip side of that coin, though, sole proprietors have the full burden of responsibility should their business fail.

That means that, unlike what happens with LLCs, debt collectors would be able to hold them personally liable without any kind of limit should their business fail.

If a sole proprietorship can be considered an alternative to a single-member LLC, a general partnership can be considered to be for a multi-member LLC-member LLC. A general partnership usually has at least two partners who share equal liability for their business. That means that those partners divide their profits, costs, losses, and expenses equally. The same applies to the work they have to do for their partnership. Of course, the more partners a general partnership has, the wider and deeper its pool of investors and expertise will naturally become.

Then there are C corporations. C corporations are subject to double taxation. That means both the income of C corporations and the income of the individuals who are shareholders of those corporations are taxed. This is something that makes C corporations unappealing to some, but this model is not without its advantages. For instance, C corporations are required to pay dividends on company earnings. Similarly, losses that C corporations suffer do not get passed onto their owners and shareholders. However, it should be noted that this also means C corporation owners are not allowed to claim any tax benefits for their losses, if and when they occur.

If you are looking for an alternative to LLCs with distinct tax benefits, then S corporations might be the way to go. S corporations have, at most, 100 owners, all of whom are subject to limited liability. These owners are taxed on their personal income levels, the way general partnerships are. Some S corporations are subject to corporate tax, which is a tax that is imposed on the capital or income of corporations. Whether or not an S corporation is subject to such a tax depends on what state it is in (Kagan, 2021).

S corporations are not the only entities that allow for certain tax benefits. Limited partnerships, for instance, can help their owners avoid self-employment taxes (Chaves, n.d.). A limited partnership is a business that has co-owners. All or some of these co-owners might be limited partners, meaning that they can enjoy limited liability protection. If that is the case for a co-owner, then that means that their liability is limited to the amount that they originally invested. Logically, the more people invest in a limited partnership, the more profits get divided. So, the owners of a limited liability company would end up investing more and obtaining smaller profits than they might have liked.

WHY SHOULD YOU CHOOSE A MULTI-MEMBER LLC OVER A SINGLE-MEMBER ONE?

The most obvious—and therefore likely most easily over-looked—alternative to a single-member LLC is a multi-member one. After all, multi-member LLCs offer their owners the exact same benefits as single-member LLCs.

Both are equally flexible and simple when it comes to managing and forming them. The key difference between them, which might make multi-member LLCs the more appealing option out of the two, is this: if you start a single-member LLC, you will be the sole person liable for your business and any debts it might incur. However, if you start a multi-member LLC, then that liability will be shared equally between you and your partners.

Of course, the same thing goes for any profits that your multi-member LLC turns in. Those profits will be divided equally among all co-owners. So, if you want a format where you get to keep all of the profits, then this might make a multi-member LLC-member LLC suboptimal for you. Then again, you might reconsider just how suboptimal this option is once you discover that multi-member LLC owners do not have to pay self-employment taxes, which can be hefty, as mentioned before. This, combined with the fact that multi-member LLCs are eligible for certain kinds of tax deductions and credits that single-member LLCs simply are not eligible for, might make you warm up to the idea of them (UpCounsel, n.d.-b).

What you have to do if you are trying to decide between single-member LLCs and multi-member LLCs (and any other business entities, really) is to consider what you want and need. Do you want the simplest possible business model? If so, then you should choose a single-member LLC over a multi-member LLC, because the latter is a bit more complicated to run, given that there are more people involved in it. Do you want to avoid self-employment taxes and share your liability with others? If that is the case, then you might want to go with a multi-member LLC.

IN SUMMARY

Thinking about your wants and needs and figuring out which kind of corporation suits you the most is the only way to create a business that you love and will succeed at. If you want to make your business a true success, though, then you have to know that there are certain "dos and don'ts" that go with forming an LLC. This way, you can keep taking the best steps possible for your LLC and avoid a great many mistakes. But before we take a closer look at these dos and don'ts, let us go over the risks that LLCs pose, just so that you can be sure you are starting off on the right foot:

- Single-member LLCs offer flexibility and simplicity, but also come with specific disadvantages.
- One of the biggest risks of owning a single-member LLC is that their owners are personally liable for the business' debts and obligations.
- Another major risk is that raising capital for a single member LLC might be difficult.
- Single-member LLCs are subject to self-employment taxes, which can become a significant expense.
- Lastly, single-member LLCs are not eligible for certain tax deductions and credits that some other types of corporations are.

8

THE DOS AND DON'TS OF FORMING AN LLC

As simple a process as forming an LLC is, there are some things that you need to consider once you have officially started the process. This includes all kinds of things, from choosing your business name to picking the business structure that is best for you. Doing your research properly and using the right resources is important for this, if you want to avoid the various pitfalls you can come across when you are setting up your business. What exactly are those pitfalls, then, and what are the things you should absolutely do and avoid doing if you want to be able to leap over them?

THE ESSENTIAL DO'S

Before you take any steps to form your LLC, you must first **make sure that you understand all the advantages, risks, and disadvantages that come with LLCs.** Depending on what kind of LLC you are forming—single member, multi member or hybrid—you must also understand the advantages and risks that go with them as well. Otherwise, you cannot make an informed decision. It is important that you **consult a business attorney** to better understand the risks you may be facing in your business venture. You should also consult such an attorney if and when you run into any problems while running your LLC or if you are unsure about how to proceed with any legal matter for your business.

One of the first things you will have to do when forming an LLC is choose a name for your business. This is true regardless of whether you are starting a single-member LLC or a multi-member one. It is important that you do your research and do it well when naming your LLC. That means you need to **check if the name you have chosen for your business has already been taken.** This will require going onto your state's database and looking through the names registry. While you are doing that, it is important that you **work on a list of backup names** and secondary options that you can use if your first choice has already been taken off the market. You can keep this list by your side as you go through the state database. That way you can immediately see if the ones on your list are available, should you discover that your first choice is not.

The next thing you need to do is **have a written operating agreement** at hand. You are usually not required to have an operating agreement to form your LLC, as you have seen. However, that does not mean you should not have one, even if your LLC is a single-member one. Your operating agreement is something that will define and lay out all the details of how your business will be run. As such, it can help you avoid a great deal of confusion and disagreements (like ownership disputes for instance) in the near or distant future (Incorporation Guru, n.d.).

To quickly recap, your operating agreement needs to include the following information (United States Small Business Administration, n.d.):

- The percentage of each member's ownership if the entity is a multi-member LLC
- Each member's voting rights and responsibilities
- Each member and manager's duties, obligations and powers
- How profits and losses are to be distributed among members
- How and how often meetings will be conducted
- What the buy-sell and buyout rules are
- What the general rules of management are

- How dissolution will be dealt with, if and when the LLC is dissolved
- Who your replacement will be in the event of your departure from the LLC or death
- Your signature as the owner of the LLC

As per the last step of forming your LLC, you have to **set up a separate bank account for your LLC**. The importance of this cannot be overstated, seeing as failure to do so can put your personal assets at risk in the event that your LLC is sued or gets into some kind of debt. While you are setting up that account, you might also want to get a separate credit card in your LLC's name. That way you can make doubly sure that your personal and business assets don't mix and that LLC-related expenses go on the card they are supposed to go on (Joseph & Joseph & Hanna, n.d.).

As previously touched upon, you will need to **file an annual report**—or bi-annual or tri-annual report—after you have officially formed your LLC. The requirements you have to fulfill for filing an annual report can change from state to state. Given that, you should check your secretary of state's website to find out what those requirements are in advance. Some states, such as Ohio, will not require you to file annual reports but bi-annual or tri-annual ones instead. States that do this, however, will ask you to fill out something called a Statement of Information. States use these Statements of Information to keep track of which companies are still conducting business in their territories (UpCounsel, n.d.-b).

In your annual report, you will typically have to provide the following information (Horwitz, 2022):

- Your LLC's name and EIN
- Your LLC's address
- Your LLC number, which is assigned to you after you have registered your business
- What your LLC's purpose for doing business is
- The names of each LLC member and their addresses
- The name and physical address of your LLC's registered agent
- Authorized signatures

Not filing your annual report or not filing it on time is a poor idea, as it comes with penalties and other unwanted consequences. This is why your state will typically send you reminders that you need to file your report a little before you are supposed to file it. If you miss your deadline, your state will first send you a reminder about this. If you still fail to file your report, though, then your state might charge late fees and take away the limited liability protection that your LLC had afforded you, which can open you up to some unwanted financial obligations and even dissolve your LLC. This final consequence is typically a last result though.

The problem with failing to file your annual report is that it causes your LLC to lose its good standing with its state. This can push the state to make your LLC pay late fees, outstanding payments, and taxes for missed years immediately, if you want your business to retain its ability to conduct operations as it normally would.

The good news about annual reports is that they are not hard to file at all, and neither are they very difficult to fill out, considering how simple the information you have to provide in them is. You can file your annual reports both by snail mail and online, from the comfort of your own home these days.

While you are at it, you should also make sure you create a solid business plan. Your business plan is something that can give your LLC a sense of direction, as you have seen. It can also make the process of raising capital for your LLC easier, as individuals and institutions that are likely to extend you credit will want to see one.

Another thing you need to do once you have formed and started managing your LLC is to **keep very thorough records**. As usual the kinds of documents you have to keep records of vary from state to state. Some states do not even have any record keeping requirements! Keeping records, though, is something you should still do, even if you are in such a state. It is just good business practice, after all.

The kinds of documents you should keep to comply with your state requirements and for the sake of good business practice are (Haskins, 2022a):

- **Formation documents.** Your formation documents are copies of your articles of organization that you had filed to form your LLC and the certification of formation you were given as a result. They can also include any documents that confirm you have made any amendments you might have made to your original formation documents and ones that confirm you have registered your business in other, additional states.

- **Operating Agreement.** Your operating agreement is obviously very important, as it contains details about how your business will be run. It also contains information about how your business will be dissolved, should things come to that. Having this information on hand is a sound business practice that can help you avoid headaches later on.

- **A complete and Updated List of LLC Managers and Members.** You should always keep a list of the managers and members making up your LLC. You should update it regularly. This does not just mean writing down the names of the people who join or leave your business. It also means keeping their contact information—meaning their email and phone numbers—as well as physical addresses on file.

- **Meeting Notes and Resolutions.** You should keep thorough records of each and every business meeting that takes place following the formation of your

LLC. This includes everything that is discussed in meetings and any decisions that are arrived at at the end.

- **All Permits and Licenses**. You should keep copies of all local and state permits and licenses.
- **Insurance Information**. Once you have gotten the business insurance you need, you should keep both the insurance policies in question and the contact information of your insurance company on file.
- **Contracts**. Hold onto each and every contract that your LLC has been a part of. This includes but is not limited to nondisclosure agreements, employment contracts, supplier contracts, and leases.
- **Employment Tax Records**. Employment tax records should be kept for four of you at the very least, as per IRS rules and regulations. These records include W-4 forms, essential information about your employees, the dates they started their employment, any and all time cards, and records of all payments made to employees.
- **Tax Records**. The IRS expects all taxpayers to hold onto their tax records for three years. This is because the IRS is given three years to begin any kind of audit. It is a good idea, though, to hold onto your tax records for up to seven years. Your tax records include all tax returns, invoices, paid bills, canceled checks, and the like.

There are a couple of other things that you should do after you have formed your LLC that will help you manage it better. These are to find yourself a good accountant, create an effective business website for marketing and branding purposes, get business insurance, and get the licenses and permits that you need to get (Truic, n.d.-a). In doing all this, you can increase your LLC's effectiveness and make sure you are complying with all local, state, and federal laws that are applicable to your business.

THE ESSENTIAL DON'TS

We've covered all the dos of forming and managing an LLC. What about the don'ts? What are some of the things you should absolutely avoid doing to ensure the success of your business?

For starters, it is important that you **don't fail to keep up with local, state, and federal rules, laws, and regulations**. Such legal matters are usually in constant flux. As such, it is important to stay current, do research, and keep track of these kinds of things. Having a good business attorney on hand can help a great deal with this, as they can instruct you on any changes and fill you in on any new requirements you have to meet.

You also **should not assume the business structure you chose in one state will automatically work in another** (My USA Corporation, 2017). The rules and regulations pertaining to LLCs can change from state to state, as we have seen over and over. Different states, for instance, can offer different tax incentives to different kinds of corporations. An incentive that might exist for an LLC in, say, Ohio might not exist for one in New York. As such, you should make an effort to be aware of the regulations for the state you live in. You should also look up differences in regulations, if you are moving your business from one state to another.

As you are forming your LLC, you **must not forget to bring any of the paperwork required to register your LLC**. Similarly, you should not forget to bring the filing and registration fees. Failing to bring these things will mean failing to register and form you LLC. This might delay the process of starting your business.

One thing you should **avoid doing at all costs is to personally guarantee any obligations or debts in writing or verbally** unless you actually intend to be personally responsible for your LLC's debts and obligations. Giving such a guarantee would render the limited liability protection you are afforded fairly ineffective (Joseph & Joseph & Hanna, n.d.). You should similarly **avoid fraudulently conveying your assets** if and when your LLC is ever sued. Fraudulently converting your assets can mean one of two things (Reuting, 2016):

- Selling or transferring assets below market value as this would defraud your creditors

- Transferring business assets to your personal assets in an effort to protect them under limited liability laws.

Fraudulent conveyance is something you need to absolutely avoid because it is considered a civil offense. This means that the penalty for this behavior can be a lot worse than handing over your business assets in the long run.

The same can be said of **tax evasion**, as doing so can get you into a heap of trouble. Tax evasion obviously means dodging taxes you have to pay through illegal means. It, however, is not the same thing as tax avoidance, which is perfectly legal. The scary thing about tax evasion is that it is actually a criminal offense. The famous gangster Al Capone wasn't imprisoned after all for the many crimes, such as murder, that he had committed. He was imprisoned for tax evasion. So while you may look into legal tax avoidance strategies by consulting your accountant, you absolutely should not engage in tax evasion.

Lastly, **if your business engages in international transactions, you must not skip out on filing your foreign transactions with the state.**

COMMON PITFALLS TO AVOID WHEN FORMING AN LLC

Running an LLC comes with specific pitfalls. Falling into one can be rather easy—that is, if you don't know what to watch out for. An all-too-common pitfall is thinking that your business is not big enough to be an LLC. This is an erroneous belief, though, especially since single-member LLCs are a thing. The problem with this line of thinking is that it can cause you to fall into the wrong kind of mindset, where you are working to grow your business before it is ready. Growth can be a great thing, but it is something that should be done when the time is right. If you try to grow your LLC too quickly before you have perfected the products and services you are offering and made sure that they are of top quality, then the odds of your business failing will increase. This is why it's a bad idea to equate success with how big your company is at a given moment.

In keeping with that logic, thinking that your business is big enough for you to set up an LLC is also a bad idea. Just because a business has become profitable, does not mean it is ready to become a limited liability company. Whether or not you are ready to incorporate a business, then, depends on more than its scale. This is especially true if you haven't taken stock of your finances to see if you can take on the burden that incorporating may bring by making you invest some of your assets in your company or in the form of taxes. Before you start the process of launching your LLC, think carefully about whether you are ready to do so in both the long and short term. Make sure that you understand all the requirements, obligations, and consequences that forming an LLC comes with, and only take on that responsibility if you feel that you are ready for it.

Another exceedingly common pitfall where LLCs are concerned is failing to file the proper paperwork. If you don't file the correct paperwork when forming and managing an LLC, then you will have to face certain consequences. At best, you may be delayed in forming your LLC, as the secretary of state might not accept your incomplete documents. At worst, you may incur penalties or even be forced to dissolve your LLC if, for instance, you forget to file your annual report. The same goes for not getting the permits and licenses you need to run your business on time.

Lots of people try to form and manage their LLCs without getting a proper business lawyer. This, however, is decidedly a mistake. True, going online and getting the forms you need to start your LLC without getting any legal assistance is quite easy to do. But it is not all that wise. The fact of the matter is, a good business lawyer can help you with a number of things, including managing important disagreements with business partners if you are starting a multi-member LLC; figuring out how to manage your relationships with your investors, if you have them; and figuring out how to expand your business so that it is operational in multiple states (McDowell, 2019). Working without a good business attorney can also make it harder for you to keep track of any relevant changes to state legislation that might be relevant to your LLC. Not keeping track of such changes is a common pitfall that can cause an array of problems for LLCs.

Of course, the biggest and most obvious pitfall that an LLC owner might fall into is choosing the wrong options for their business. As we have seen, there are a lot of options that LLC owners can consider and choose from when they are forming their business. Should they go with a single member or multi-member entity? Should they form their LLC in this state or that one over there? Should they look for investors or get a loan from a bank? All of these questions and more are things future LLC owners need to carefully consider before founding their businesses. Otherwise, they might end up making the wrong choices, which could hinder the growth of their business. Such choices can also impact their ability to reap benefits that would otherwise have been available to them. Finding out that your LLC could have been eligible for certain tax benefits if you had formed it in New Jersey, rather than New York is sure to dampen anyone's mood, after all.

IN SUMMARY

Forming an LLC is a simple process. But it is also rife with potential pitfalls. These pitfalls can be avoided, though, if you make sure you do certain things and avoid certain others at all costs. Whether you fall into any pitfalls or not, there may come a time when you conclude that dissolving your LLC is the right thing to do for you. It is important that you know how to go about doing that correctly and without having to deal with any unnecessary hassle, as you will see in the following chapter. If you want to avoid having to dissolve by making a big mistake, though, going over the numerous dos and don'ts of forming and managing LLCs one last time is probably a good idea:

- It is important that you do your research and thus avoid common pitfalls when you are forming your LLC.
- Some common pitfalls include failing to file the necessary paperwork, thinking your LLC is licensed without getting your license, and forgetting to keep your LLC up to date.
- Consulting with a business attorney can help you navigate the process and ensure that everything is done correctly.

9

DISSOLVING YOUR LLC

T here might be any number of reasons why you want to close your LLC. Maybe your business is not doing as well as you had hoped. Maybe you are finally ready to retire in comfort. Whatever your reasons might be, knowing the steps you need to take as you go about dissolving your LLC, such as canceling your licenses or transferring power to another individual, is important. So is knowing when you should close your LLC.

SIGNS THAT IT IS TIME TO CLOSE YOUR LLC

Human beings are born with the instinct to fight on. We often struggle in the face of hardship. While this is a good, admirable quality to have, sometimes it is important to know when to stop. It is important to know when to look at the company you have created with your own hands and say, "I am done," for both your sake and even your business's sake. To that end, you need to know what some of the signs indicating you should close your LLC are, because there are many.

The first and probably clearest sign that you need to dissolve your LLC is if you are losing money or not making any more money. In such cases, you might have the instinct to keep going. You might be inclined to say, take out a loan, so that you can push on. A loan, however, can only be a temporary solution, a bandaid in such cases. It can keep your company going for a short while longer, but eventually, that money will run out. When it does, you will, more often than not, find yourself in the uncomfortable position of seeing that your business is still losing money and being unable to pay your loan back. This might result in you having to close your business anyway, except this time on someone else's terms rather than your own (Businessify, 2020).

This same thing goes if you are not making as much money as you expected, want, or need. Even if your LLC is profitable enough to keep supporting you and your family, this is a good sign that you should close up shop. This is doubly true for cases where you keep making a profit, but that profit is getting smaller and smaller with each passing year, despite your best efforts. Under these kinds of circumstances, letting go can understandably be difficult. But it is important that you do so and "quit while you are ahead," so to speak. After all, the whole point of starting your own business was to make money. So why stick with a business that is no longer able to meet that goal? Think of it this way: closing a company before you start incurring losses can allow you to stop with no small amount of savings in your pocket. You can then use part of those savings to launch another LLC if you so desire. If you stick with your current company though? Well, things may get even worse as a result, and you may find that you are now losing money and have to stop when you could have stopped with some money in your pocket.

While making money is important given the kind of world we live in, sticking with a job or business that makes you unhappy is not really worth it. If the business you are in no longer interests you and fails to make you happy, then do you really want to keep sticking with it? Yes, running a business is supposed to make you a lot of money. But it is also supposed to provide you with some degree of satisfaction. It is supposed to be fun! If it is not, if going to work is miserable or boring for you, then, honestly? What's really stopping you from walking away?

Your health should always be your priority, even above your work. If you find that your health is suffering because of your work, then it is vital that you step away from your business so that you can focus on your health. Your work should not wear your body and immune system down to such a degree that you cannot enjoy the fruits of your labor. It should not be contributing to debilitating mental health problems, such as chronic anxiety or depression. If either of these cases is applicable to you, then at the very, very least you need to temporarily step back from your business and re-evaluate how you want to continue managing it. It would be better, though, if you were to evaluate whether or not you should go back to work.

Before making any kind of decision, though, take a moment to look at your business and your own work patterns and habits closely. Is there anything you can do or change to alleviate some of the stress you have been under? Can you, perhaps, start delegating some of the responsibilities that you have been dealing with? Can you cut back on your work hours and impose a rule where you are not dealing with work after a certain hour? These might be very simple solutions, but you would be surprised at how effective they can be in helping you to reduce your stress and anxiety levels. That said, if you have evaluated all these things and concluded that it would be better for your physical and mental health if you were to stop? Then that is absolutely what you should do.

The same logic applies to aging. As we age, our bodies objectively become weaker and frailer. Sure, the effects of aging can be slowed down to a degree through healthy eating and working out. But even the healthiest 80-year-old man cannot keep working at the same pace he used to work when he was in his twenties. All that to say, if you are getting to be a certain age and are therefore slowing down, you might want to consider closing down your LLC. You should remember that running a business takes a significant amount of both mental and physical energy. It requires a lot of stamina too, and we start running low on both of these things as we age. If this is the case for you, then it is probably time to take a cue from your own body and slow things down.

Another common sign is wanting to pursue other interests. Some people might not think that this is a good enough reason to dissolve an LLC. However, they would be wrong. If you have been running an LLC for a while and if you feel that you have accomplished all that you wanted to accomplish, why should not you stop? Why keep sticking with a venture when you are clearly ready to move on? If you were to dissolve your LLC at this point could start another venture in another industry you are interested in, for example. You could also take some much-needed and well-deserved time off and rest.

In contrast to this latter case, you might sometimes find yourself in a position where you are unable to meet the goals that you set for yourself when you started your business. Yes, this too indicates that you can dissolve your LLC and wrap things up. Being unable to meet your goals despite striving to do so can be indicative of numerous things. It might mean, for example, that the goals you set for yourself were unrealistic and therefore impossible to meet, to begin with.

It might mean that the market you are in has changed in such a way that it makes it impossible for you to meet your goals. Whatever the case may be, there are two things you could do in this situation. The first is to re-evaluate your goals and the market. Do you really think you can adjust and change your goals so that you can change this situation? Do you think you truly have the physical, emotional, and psychological energy you need to make such changes? If you answer these questions with a "no," then there will be only one thing left for you to do: close your LLC.

Not being able to get enough customers to keep you going is a valid reason for dissolving your LLC as well. Businesses depend on their customers for their longevity and survival. Not having enough customers means not being able to survive for very long. So why not choose to stop yourself before this circumstance forces you to do so anyway? Before you decide to dissolve your LLC, though, you should first see if you can change up your marketing strategy and efforts to see if you can acquire more customers over time. If you can, then you obviously will not have to quit your business. If, on the other hand, the conclusion you draw is that all the marketing strategies in the world will not be able to help you? Well, you know what that means in that case.

Another factor that determines the survival of a business is its employees. They are the ones that do the work necessary to keep a company running, after all. But what if, despite your best efforts, you cannot find any good employees?

What if you are constantly struggling to find qualified candidates for the positions you are advertising? What if you have a low retention rate because of this—or employees that you do find are too difficult to work with? If this situation goes on for a prolonged period of time, then it might be time to, yet again, throw in the towel.

Before you make any major decisions, though, you should first re-evaluate your hiring process and your job descriptions. Is there anything about those descriptions that you can change to better communicate your needs and the responsibilities of potential employees? Can you do anything to expand your candidate pool somehow, like reach out to other sources? Can you change up your candidate vetting process in any way? More importantly, will these help you find the kinds of employees you need and want for your business? If you think that the answer to that question is "yes," you can perhaps try for another round and see if your new strategies and solutions work. You should put a realistic time limit on that round, though. Once that time is up, you could consider dissolving your LLC if you still haven't found the kinds of candidates that you want.

A final indication to close your LLC might simply be that things are not working out. There is not always a solid, visible reason or reasons why a business is not going the way you want it to. Call it bad luck or bad timing, but whatever the case may be, if things are not working out despite your best efforts, there is no shame or blame in walking away.

THE STEPS INVOLVED IN CLOSING AN LLC

The process of closing or dissolving an LLC begins with deciding whether you need to do so or not. If you own a single-member LLC, this decision will be up to you and you alone. In such a case, you might evaluate your reasons for wanting to close and then immediately move forward once your mind has been made up. If you own a multi-member LLC, though, things will not be quite as simple as that, seeing as you will need to arrive at this decision together with the other members of your LLC. This will, in turn, require taking a vote.

When members of an LLC decide to close that LLC, they essentially partake in what's known as a "voluntary dissolution" (Watts, 2022). During voluntary dissolution, all members cast a vote either in favor of or against this course of action. The process kicks in either when a member calls for a vote or if a business partner passes away, unless the LLC's operating agreement covers what needs to be done should such an event happen. That, as you will remember, is just one of the reasons why having an operating agreement is important, but let us not digress. The votes are counted once every member has voted, and the majority decision is adhered to, which may or may not be to dissolve the LLC.

In some cases, an LLC owner might want to step down from their position, rather than close down their LLC entirely. If this is the case, then they will have to transfer their ownership to someone else rather than proceed with dissolution. The rules for transferring ownership are typically covered in the operating agreement, or at least they should be. Even if they are not, the transfer process usually works in one of two ways: either the owner is bought out or they sell their LLC (Kaminsky, 2022).

There may be specific provisions for buying out a member's share, which again are usually noted in an operating agreement. If transfer rules are not specified in this agreement, then you should know that some states require that the LLC in question be completely dissolved. If no such requirements are being imposed by the state, then either another member of the business or the LLC itself buys out the shares of the departing member. To that end, the two parties have to determine the worth of those shares. Then the LLC or another member pays the departing member that sum. Of course, this entire process has to be approved by the other members of the LLC.

Alternatively, an LLC owner might transfer their power to someone else by selling their LLC. The terms of the sale are determined by the two parties—they don't have to be specified in the operating agreement. Once both parties are satisfied with those terms, they memorialize them in a change of ownership letter or a preliminary memorandum. The ownership agreement then goes into effect, much like any other business contract would.

Going back to the dissolution process, let us say that an owner has decided to close your LLC and that the other LLC members, if there are any, agree with their decision. In that case, the next step is to file the final tax returns. A number of states only allow an LLC to be dissolved once the state is able to verify that they are in good standing with the state tax agency. They allow the LLC to file their dissolution paperwork only after this phase is complete (Watts, 2022). An LLC owner will know that they have received the tax clearance they need when a certificate or letter indicating as much is given to them. This is why it indicates that the tax return you are filing is the last one you will ever file. All that being said, filing all your final tax returns—both state and federal ones—is very important, even if you are not required to do so by your state. Otherwise, you will run the risk of becoming personally liable for unpaid payroll taxes.

When you are finished with those pesky taxes, the next step will be filing an article of dissolution. An article of dissolution is an official document wherein you ask your state to dissolve your LLC. It can easily be found on the website of your secretary of state. Depending on the website, the document may be referred to as a certificate of cancellation or a certificate of dissolution. Whatever this form is referred to as, when you are filling it out, you will usually provide information about your LLC, such as how many members make up your business. The articles may also have you declare whether or not you have distributed your assets.

To file your articles of dissolution, you will usually have to pay a small fee, just as you did when you filed your articles of organization. Since this fee can vary from state to state, you should check your secretary of state's website to find out the exact amount. You should also check and see if your state requires you to file any additional paperwork, which some states do. Once your articles of dissolution have been approved, you will be given a certificate of dissolution which you should keep in your records.

Before you file your articles of dissolution, though, you will need to notify your creditors that your LLC is no longer in operation. "Creditors" refers to leaders, insurance carriers, service providers, suppliers, and the like (Watts, 2022). You can go about notifying your creditors by sending them a formal notice via certified mail. This notice should include a deadline for your creditors to submit a claim and a statement saying that should their claim arrive after that date, they will be barred (Steingold, 2013). It should also include a mailing address to which the creditor should send their claim. In the case of your suppliers, it should include a final delivery date. The deadline for a creditor to submit a claim is usually something between 90 and 180 days. In most states, it is 120 days (Steingold, 2013). In addition to all of that, some states may require you to publish a notice in the local newspaper. Without notifying creditors that your LLC is dissolving, their claim may survive the dissolution. This means that you may find yourself having to settle a debt after that 90-180 days period is up. By publishing your notice, though, you can mitigate this risk significantly.

Having done all that, you will now have to pay any and all outstanding debts, assuming your creditors sent their claims by the deadline you provided. The debts you will have to settle can be anything from credit card balances to loans. If you find that you are unable to pay these debts, then you might want to consider selling off a number of your assets so that you can raise the funds you need. That brings us to the next phase, which is distributing your remaining assets. You should only move onto this phase after you are done paying all your taxes and settling all your debts. You can then take stock of what's left. Your remaining assets will typically be things like profits, investments, and even tangible goods, like any products you used to sell. When you are done taking inventory of your remaining assets, you can divide them among the LLC members. How these assets will be divided should have been covered in... you guessed it, your operating agreement.

Even distributing all your remaining assets is not the end of this process, however. There are three steps left, the first being terminating any and all licenses and permits you had gotten for your LLC. This includes but is not limited to local licenses, as well as state and federal ones. You might think that dealing with this step sounds like an unnecessary headache but failing to cancel them can become an even greater source of pain. This is because that failure can lead to your being slammed with certain penalties, which you probably don't want to deal with.

The second to last thing you need to do is notify the IRS that your business has been dissolved. This can be done by sending a copy of your articles of dissolution to the IRS, along with a formal letter stating that your LLC has been dissolved and is no longer in operation. You should also be sure that you filed a final return and all accompanying forms, made your final federal tax deposits, and reported employment taxes. To do so, you will need to file form 941, otherwise known as the Employer's Quarterly Federal Tax Return, or form 944, known as the Employer's Annual Federal Tax Return. Finally, you must cancel your EIN and close your IRS business account. To do so, you make sure the letter you sent to the IRS includes the following information (Internal Revenue Service, n.d.):

- Your LLC's full, legal name
- Your LLC's EIN
- Your LLC's business address
- Your reason for dissolving your business

The final step now is to wrap everything up and wind down. This means taking care of things like letting go of your employees and providing them with severance packages if they are owed them, negotiating the cancellation of any contracts you held, and informing your customers about when your last day of business will be.

TIPS FOR DISSOLVING YOUR LLC

Now that we have gone over how to properly dissolve your LLC, here are a couple of important tidbits that you should be aware of as you move through the process:

- If you have registered your business in more than one state, you will have to file your articles of dissolution in each and every one of those states. If you do not, you will run the risk of being subjected to various state and local taxes and penalties. You will even be expected to keep filing your annual reports, even if there is nothing to report on, and may incur a fine for failing to do so.
- This process that we covered is for voluntary dissolutions, as you probably surmised. There are cases, however, where your LLC may be dissolved without your initiating it. These cases are known as involuntary dissolutions and they can be categorized in one of two ways: administrative dissolution and judicial dissolution. An administrative dissolution is one that is imposed by the secretary of state, whereas a judicial one is issued by a court of law. The former might happen if you have failed to file your annual reports or to maintain a registered agent. The latter might happen if, say, there's too much disagreement going on between the different members of a multi-

member LLC or there has been misconduct of some kind on the part of at least one of the members.

- Regardless of whether or not an LLC is being dissolved voluntarily or involuntarily, the process itself does not change.
- The amount of time it takes for an LLC to be properly dissolved varies from state to state. Usually, though, it should take between one and two weeks. If complications arise in the form of unknown creditors making claims, for instance, or assets being liquidated, then those two weeks can very easily become six. If you are willing to pay for a business attorney, though, that period of time can be shortened.
- Consulting with a business attorney while managing the dissolution process is not a requirement. However, it is a generally recommended business practice that can come in very handy in the event that complications do arise.

IN SUMMARY

Since you now know all there is to know about forming, managing, and even dissolving an LLC, it can officially be said that you know almost everything there is to know about this business entity. Before we wrap things up though, let us quickly summarize the dissolution process, seeing as you might be feeling like a ton of information has just been dropped on you:

- If you are going to close your LLC, you need to first figure out what your reason for doing so is and see if dissolving your business is the best course of action for you to take.
- If and when you do decide to dissolve your LLC, you will need to file all the necessary paperwork with the secretary of state's office and pay any outstanding debts you may have and all the fees you are expected to pay.

Put like that, the process does not seem quite as daunting as before, now does it?

Spread the Word!

I've written the guide that I wished had been available when I first started out... and you can help me get it to more people.

Simply by sharing your honest opinion of this book on Amazon, you'll show new business owners where they can find all the information they need to take the headache out of the LLC process.

Please scan the QR-code to go straight to the review page.

Thank you for your support. This process doesn't have to be as difficult as it seems when you first get into it – and I can't wait for more people to know that.

CONCLUSION

Starting a business–any kind of business—can understandably be a daunting process. There are a myriad of things to consider when you are thinking of launching your own company, starting with what kind of business entity you should go with. If you want to adopt a very simple and flexible business model, though—one that can afford you numerous tax benefits and deductions—the answer to that question is an LLC. But knowing that an LLC might be a good option for you does not mean you can just dive into the process of starting one with a blindfold on. The plain truth is, if you want your business to succeed, you need to really understand how to form your LLC, how you can structure and manage it, and what the advantages and even disadvantages of the structure you have chosen are. Only once you know these things can you confidently figure out exactly what you need to do to make your business a success.

The good news is that now that you have finished reading *LLCs for Beginners*, you can go about doing just that. After all, you are no longer in the dark as to what precisely an LLC is. You also know, for instance, that the personal assets of the owner of a limited liability company are afforded a degree of protection, so long as they keep those assets separate from their business ones.

Actually, since having a ton of information chucked your way all at once can be a little overwhelming, let us quickly go over all that you have learned and gained in reading *LLCs for Beginners*.

For starters, now that you have finished this book, you know how to gauge whether an LLC is right for you. You know how to consider the various advantages and disadvantages that LLCs come with, such as affording you limited liability protection and being difficult to raise funds for, respectively. You also know which questions you need to ask yourself to best determine your current financial abilities and business goals. These questions can help you grasp your needs better, which will enable you to conclude that an LLC really is right for you.

Once you have confidently chosen the LLC model, you can go about forming your business, which is an incredibly simple and easy process. Not only that, it does not require a great deal of money and, therefore, won't break the bank. To form an LLC, you will need to follow a set of steps that begin with registering your LLC name and end with creating a bank account for your business. You don't have to be a citizen of the United States to be able to form an LLC or even have an office space. You can launch one from the comfort of your own home or work from a coffee shop, so long as you have a registered agent with a physical address in the state your business is in.

Before you can file the forms you need to file so that you can start your LLC, you will naturally need to decide whether you want a single-member LLC or a multi-member one. If you decide on a multi-member one, you will have to further consider your options as you try to choose between member-managed and manager-managed multi-member LLCs. Luckily, you will already be aware of the fact that single-member LLCs are simpler to manage than multi-member ones, have fewer requirements that you need to meet, and give you the ability to deduct your business expenses from your personal taxes. You will also be aware of how the fact that you will have complete control over your LLC means you will be the only one responsible for its success or failure. This awareness will lead you to make the best possible choice, depending on what your needs and wants are.

Having formed your LLC, you will move on to the process of running it, which, again, should seem much less intimidating now that you have a handle on what you need to do. You will start by familiarizing yourself with all the state and federal laws your LLC has to comply with. You will then file any and all necessary paperwork as required by those laws and regulations, such as your annual reports. Obviously, you will need to pay your LLCs income tax too.

Speaking of taxes, having discovered all the minutiae concerning them, you will know exactly how to tackle tax season as well. Now that you are aware that LLCs are taxed as pass-through entities, for instance, you will pay your taxes on the LLCs income on your personal tax returns. You will be able to have your LLC taxed as a C corporation or an S corp, if you so choose, deduct business expenses in various ways, and pay self-employment taxes. Obviously, you won't skip out on paying any federal, state, or local taxes during this process.

You will even be able to handle the process of dissolving your LLC in the event that you decide you want or need to. The most important takeaway you will walk away from after having read *LLCs for Beginners*, though, is knowing how to start your LLC or even if it's time to close it. You are now able to decide whether forming an LLC at this particular moment is the right decision to make for you. If you do, then you will have all that you need and more to launch your very own limited liability company.

GLOSSARY

Annual report: a report that provides basic information about a limited liability company, like its name, address, and the name and address of its registered agent, as well as that of its members and managers.

Anonymous LLC: a limited liability company whose owners, members, or managers are kept anonymous, thereby minimizing the legal liability they are under.

Articles of organization: the formal, legal documents that need to be filed with the state to establish a limited liability company.

Asset: anything of economic value to a business, such as cash, patents, machinery, and buildings.

Bank statement: a digital or printed record of a business's bank account, showing the amount that has been put into it and taken out of it on a monthly basis.

Business entity: an organization that has been officially formed so that it can conduct business.

Business expense: the cost it takes to keep operating a business and the expenses made to that end.

Business interruption insurance: a type of insurance coverage that can replace the loss of income in the event that a business is interrupted after receiving some kind of damage because of a catastrophic incident, like a fire.

Business plan: a document that lays out a business's goals, strategies, and how it will achieve them.

Buyout: monetarily acquiring the shares of a limited liability company member.

C corporation: any kind of business entity or corporation that is taxed separately from its owner.

Capital: the sum total of any financial assets that a business needs to produce its goods and services.

Certificate of dissolution: a certificate that is filed with the state indicating that an LLC no longer wishes to continue its operations.

Claim: a formal request for compensation made by a creditor, such as an investor or insurance company, to recover the loss.

Collateral: any asset that a business entity or individual uses to secure a loan.

Corporate income tax: a kind of tax that is directly imposed on the capital or income of a corporation

Corporation: a large company or group of companies that can act as a single business entity.

Creditor: a person or entity that a limited liability company owed some amount of money to.

Dissolution: the process of dissolving or closing a limited liability company (or any other kind of corporation.)

Dividend: the total amount of money that a limited liability company regularly pays to its shareholders.

Doing Business As (DBA): a company that operates under a different name than the one that it was officially registered as.

Domain name: the website address of a business.

Domestic LLC: an LLC that is formed in the home state of its owner.

Double taxation: having to pay taxes on both your personal income and that of your company.

Election effective date: the date when something takes effect, such as a change in a corporation's type for tax purposes.

Employee Identification Number (EIN): a nine-digit number given to a limited liability company by the IRS as a form of identification, otherwise known as the Federal Employer Identification Number.

Employment tax record: the records of all wage, pension, and annuity payments made, including how much they amounted to and the dates they were made on.

Executive summary: an account summarizing the key points being made in a business plan.

Financial projection: the cash flow and profit-loss forecast that is done in a business proposal.

Foreign LLC: a limited liability company that is formed in a state other than the home state of the LLC owner and members.

Funding request: a written request, typically included in a business proposal, asking for funding from an investor or creditor to launch or conduct a business.

General Partnership: a basic form of partnership under US law, created through mutual agreement.

Gross profit: the sum of all earnings, profits, and interest payments for a business entity.

Gross sales: the total sales of all the products or services of a company over a set period of time.

Guaranteed payment: payments made to all the members of a limited liability company for services rendered.

I-9: a form that verifies that an individual is eligible to be employed within a country.

Income tax: the tax that an individual has to pay based on their income.

Incorporate: the act of forming a legal corporation.

Indemnity protection: an insurance policy that guarantees protection for any losses or damages that a policyholder incurs.

Individual taxpayer number (ITIN): a taxpayer number assigned to certain resident aliens or nonresident aliens, their spouses or dependents when the individuals in question are not able to get social security numbers.

Insurance: a kind of coverage provided to businesses to cover any potential losses they may suffer in the event of an accident or a disaster.

Internal Revenue Service (IRS): the revenue service of the USA, responsible for the collection of federal taxes.

Investment: the process of investing a sum in a business venture.

Involuntary dissolution: the process of the closure of an LLC.

Liability: being legally responsible for something.

Liability insurance: a kind of general insurance that protects a limited liability company in the event that it is exposed to a lawsuit or claim.

Limited liability: the shareholders of a company being legally responsible for the debts of that company to the extent of the minimum value of the shares they possess.

Limited liability company: a company whose owners are considered responsible for its debts to the extent that they invested in it.

Limited liability protection: legal protection given to the owner or members of an LLC, separating their own personal assets from the assets of their business in an effort to protect the former.

Limited partnership: a partnership that has at least one general partner (GP) and at least one limited partner.

LLC officer: an individual chosen to be in charge of day-to-day operations at a limited liability company, who serves under and reports to its members.

Loss: a decrease in the net income that a limited liability company makes.

Low-profit LLC: otherwise known as L3Cs, this is a kind of hybrid meant to attract both philanthropic and private investment to benefit society and generate profit.

Manager-managed LLC: a limited liability company that is managed by one or more chosen members.

Market analysis: the process and practice of gathering insightful information about a market.

Medicare: the U.S. government's health insurance program given to people who are 65 years old or older.

Member: the individuals or entities that have memberships of a limited liability company and are therefore considered to be its owners.

Member interest: the ownership stakes that members of a limited liability company have.

Member-managed LLC: a limited liability company that is managed by all of its members.

Multi-member limited liability company: a limited liability company that has more than one single member.

Operating agreement: an important document that limited liability companies use to lay out the responsibilities of their members and the details of how the business will be run.

Pass-through entity: a business entity where the income and profits flow through or pass through to its owners.

Paycheck: the salary or income given to an employee.

Payment allocation system: the process of paying owed profits to the members of an LLC.

Payroll taxes: a kind of tax that employers or employees have to pay, the percentage of which is calculated based on their salary.

Penalty: a payment required by some kind of government institution as a result of not meeting a legal requirement.

Pension: a steady payment made by the state to people who are over the typical retirement age, as well as to some disabled people or to widowers.

Product liability insurance: insurance given to a limited liability company to protect it against claims that its product or service damaged a customer in some way.

Professional liability insurance: coverage that will protect a limited liability company against legal claims that may arise when a customer is dissatisfied with the services you have provided.

Professional LLC (PLLC): a limited liability company formed by professionals such as doctors, accountants, or lawyers after they get a special license.

Profit: the money that a business entity has left over once it has paid all its expenses.

Property insurance: the coverage provided to a limited liability company in the event that the building and place of work is damaged enough to lead to a loss of income.

Proprietorship: the right or state of owning some kind of business or holding property.

Registered agent: an individual or entity that will receive legal documents on behalf of an LLC.

Resale license: a document certifying that you do not have to pay taxes when you purchase products wholesale to resell them to customers in the future.

Retirement account: a kind of pension that many different financial institutions provide so that an individual can save for their retirement.

Revenue: the total sum of money that a business brings in through its operations over a set period of time.

Qualified Business Income (QBI): the total amount of qualified items, means gains, losses, and deductions resulting from business transactions or trade.

S corporation: a kind of corporation where all profits, losses, credits, and deductions pass directly to owners and shareholders for federal tax purposes.

Self-employment tax: taxes that an individual pays based on their personal income if they have earned more than $400 over the tax year.

Series LLC: one limited liability company that owns smaller ones under its umbrella.

Shareholder: an individual or entity that owns shares in a limited liability company.

Single-member limited liability company: a limited liability company that only has a single member who is also the sole owner.

Small business: a firm whose revenues range between $1 million and $40 million and that has no more than 1500 employees.

Social security: a social insurance program that is made up of several different benefits, including disability, retirement, and survivor benefits.

Social Security Number (SSN): the identification number individuals are assigned with the social security program.

Sole Proprietorship: a business enterprise that is owned and run by a single individual, that provides no distinction between that individual and their business.

Tax: a mandatory, monetary contribution made to the federal, state, and sometimes local governments.

Tax avoidance: legal practices to reduce tax payments.

Tax deduction: a reduction of taxable income that is generally the result of business expenses, especially if those expenses were the result of efforts made to raise income.

Tax evasion: the illegal attempt that an individual or business makes to not pay their taxes.

Tax record: records of taxes paid and income earned.

Tax return: a form that an individual uses to declare their annual income and personal circumstances, which is then used by the IRS to determine their tax liabilities.

Transferring ownership: the process of transferring the ownership of a limited liability company to another individual or LLC.

Unit: an indication or record of ownership in a limited liability company.

Vehicle insurance: coverage provided for transport vehicles to cover losses in the event that an accident takes place.

Venture capitalism: a private equity financing that gives capital to firms and funds to start-ups, as well as to new companies if they decide that they have the potential to experience exponential growth.

Voluntary dissolution: the act and process of voluntarily dissolving, that is to say, closing, an LLC.

Voting rights: the rights that a limited liability company member has to vote on matters pertaining to business policy, such as the decision to dissolve a business.

W-2 Form: an internal IRS form that is used to report the wages employers pay to employees within a tax year.

W-4 Form: an internal IRS form that employees fill out to make their tax situation clear to their employers.

REFERENCES

AllBusiness. (2021, August 12). *10 frequently asked questions about LLCs*. Forbes. https://www.forbes.com/sites/allbusiness/2021/08/12/10-frequently-asked-questions-about-llcs/?sh=7fd33ee01595

Broussard, J. (2022, June 21). *Tax benefits of forming an LLC: Your small business guide*. Bench Accounting. https://bench.co/blog/tax-tips/llc-tax-benefits/

Buehler, N. (2022, December 22). *Can LLCs have employees?* Investopedia. https://www.investopedia.com/ask/answers/112315/can-llcs-have-employees.asp

Businessify, S. (2020, February 17). *When to shut down a business*. Small Businessify. https://smallbusinessify.com/when-to-shut-down-a-business/

Chaves, T. (n.d.). *Alternatives to an LLC*. Small Business. https://smallbusiness.chron.com/alternatives-llc-44248.html

Chen, J. (2022, April 13). *Home equity*. Investopedia. https://www.investopedia.com/terms/h/home_equity.asp

Cornell Law School. (n.d.). *franchise tax*. Legal Information Institute. https://www.law.cornell.edu/wex/franchise_tax

Corpnet. (n.d.). *Single member LLC vs multiple member LLC*. Corp Net. https://www.corpnet.com/learning-center/single-member-llc-vs-multiple-member-llc/#:~:text=Single%2Dmember%20LLC%20Ownership%20%E2%80%93%20A

DeGroot, C. A. (2020, July 1). *A few reasons why a startup should not be an LLC*. Davis Wright Tremaine. https://www.dwt.com/blogs/startup-law-blog/2020/07/a-few-reasons-why-a-startup-should-not-be-an-llc

Dock David Treece. (2018, May 29). *5 pros and 5 cons of an LLC*. Fit Small Business. https://fitsmallbusiness.com/pros-and-cons-of-an-llc/

Dropdesk. (2020, August 3). *101 inspirational quotes for startups*. The Remote Worker by DropDesk. https://drop-desk.com/blog/startup-quotes

Entrepreneur. (2008, October 16). *Co-founders of Google*. Entrepreneur. https://www.entrepreneur.com/growing-a-business/co-founders-of-google/197848

Farmiloe, B. (2022, May 23). *How to structure your business: 9 tips for structuring new businesses. Score.* https://www.score.org/resource/blog-post/how-structure-your-business-9-tips-structuring-new-businesses

Fishman, S. (n.d.-a). *Do LLC members need to be 18 years old (or older)?* Nolo. https://www.nolo.com/legal-encyclopedia/do-llc-members-need-18-years-old-older.html

Fishman, S. (n.d.-b). *What is a limited liability company (LLC)?* Nolo. https://www.nolo.com/legal-encyclopedia/what-is-a-limited-liability-company.html

Fitzpatrick, Lentz & Bubba. (2021, March 22). *Is it time to think about an LLC for Your business?* Fitzpatrick Lentz & Bubba Law. https://www.flblaw.com/is-it-time-to-think-about-an-llc-for-your-business/

Fitzpatrick, D. (n.d.). *Funding your LLC.* Nolo. https://www.nolo.com/legal-encyclopedia/funding-your-llc.html

Gellerman, E. (2021, February 10). *Everything you need to know about how to file taxes for an LLC in the U.S.* FreshBooks Blog - Resources & Advice for Small Business Owners. https://www.freshbooks.com/blog/llc-business-taxes

Haman, E. A. (2022, November 17). *Can an LLC be taxed as an S Corp.?* Legal Zoom. https://www.legalzoom.com/articles/can-an-llc-be-taxed-as-an-s-corp

Haskins, J. (2019, May 29). *How to start an LLC in 7 steps.* Legal Zoom. https://www.legalzoom.com/articles/how-to-start-an-llc-in-7-steps

Haskins, J. (2022a, May 2). *Recordkeeping for LLCs — What do you need to save?* Legal Zoom. https://www.legalzoom.com/articles/recordkeeping-for-llcs-what-do-you-need-to-save

Haskins, J. (2022b, October 30). *How to find out if a business name is taken.* Legal Zoom. https://www.legalzoom.com/articles/how-to-find-out-if-a-business-name-is-taken

Hayes, A. (2022, August 12). *Business plans: the ins and outs.* Investopedia. https://www.investopedia.com/terms/b/business-plan.asp

Horwitz, M. (2022, September 28). *Understanding the LLC annual report requirement.* LLC University®. https://www.llcuniversity.com/llc-annual-report/#:~:text=Your%20Annual%20Report%20will%20include

Huston, H. (2021, July 29). *How to form an LLC, what is an LLC, advantages disadvantages And more.* Wolters Kluwer. https://www.wolterskluwer.com/ en/expert-insights/how-to-form-an-llc-what-is-an-llc-advantages-disad vantages-and-more

Incorporation Guru. (n.d.). *How to start an LLC (and all the tips you'll need).* Incorporation Guru. https://incorporationguru.com/start-an-llc/

Insureon. (2022, July 21). *Why your LLC needs business insurance.* Insureon. https://www.insureon.com/blog/why-skimping-on-llc-insurance-can-be-a-costly-mistake

Internal Revenue Service. (n.d.). *Closing a business.* Internal Revenue Service. https://www.irs.gov/businesses/small-businesses-self-employed/closing-a-business#:~:text=You%20must%20file%20Form%20966

International Revenue Service. (n.d.). *Apply for an employer identification number (EIN) online.* Internal Revenue Service. https://www.irs.gov/busi nesses/small-businesses-self-employed/apply-for-an-employer-identifica tion-number-ein-online#:~:text=You%20may%20apply%20for%20an

Joseph & Joseph & Hanna. (n.d.). *Limited liability checklist: do's And don'ts.* Joseph & Joseph & Hanna. https://josephandjoseph.com/articles/limited-liability-checklist-dos-and-donts/

Kagan, J. (2019). *How c corporations work.* Investopedia. https://www.investope dia.com/terms/c/c-corporation.asp

Kagan, J. (2021, February 6). *Corporate tax.* Investopedia. https://www.investo pedia.com/terms/c/corporatetax.asp

Kaminsky, M. (2022, November 17). *How to transfer ownership of an LLC.* Legal Zoom. https://www.legalzoom.com/articles/how-to-transfer-ownership-of-an-llc

Kenton, W. (2021, August 22). *The truth about limited liability companies.* Investopedia. https://www.investopedia.com/terms/l/llc.asp

Knerl, L. (2020, June 15). *Single member LLC 101: everything solopreneurs need to know.* Collective Hub. https://www.collective.com/guides/single-member-llc/

Legal Zoom. (n.d.). *Registered agent services.* Legal Zoom. https://www.legal zoom.com/business/business-operations/registered-agent-overview.html

Maslow, J. (2021, April 26). *Advantages of a single member LLC.* Legal Scoops. https://www.legalscoops.com/advantages-of-a-single-member-llc/

McDowell, G. (2019, May 23). *6 common LLC creation mistakes*. Gem McDowell Law | 843-284-1021| Estate-Business-Law-Local. https://gemmcdowell.com/6-common-llc-creation-mistakes/

Municipal Association of South Carolina. (n.d.). *Business license tax*. Www.masc.sc. https://www.masc.sc/Pages/resources/Business-License-Tax.aspx#:~:text=What%20is%20a%20business%20license

Murray, J. (2021, July 21). *Capital expenses and your business taxes*. The Balance. https://www.thebalancemoney.com/capital-expenses-defined-and-explained-398153#:~:text=Capital%20expenses%20are%20costs%20associated

Murray, J. (2022a, September 13). *What is a gross receipts tax (GRT)?* The Balance. https://www.thebalancemoney.com/what-is-a-state-gross-receipts-tax-398284#:~:text=A%20gross%20receipt%20tax%20

Murray, J. (2022b, September 15). *How to change your LLC tax status to a corporation or s corporation*. The Balance. https://www.thebalancemoney.com/changing-your-llc-tax-status-to-a-corporation-or-s-corp-398989

My Company Works. (2017, March 15). *How to hire and how to pay employees LLC, Corporation, and DBA | MyCompanyWorks*. My Company Works. https://www.mycompanyworks.com/employees.htm

My USA Corporation. (2017, June 30). *Starting an LLC? Here are some do's And don'ts to be aware of*. My USA Corporation. https://www.myusacorporation.com/our-blog/2017/06/30/starting-an-llc-here-are-some-dos-and-donts-to-be-aware-of/

Nation Wide. (2020). *What is workers' compensation?* Nationwide. https://www.nationwide.com/lc/resources/small-business/articles/what-is-workers-compensation-insurance

Phelps, H. (2022, September 1). *10 tips to starting an LLC*. Market Business News. https://marketbusinessnews.com/10-tips-to-starting-an-llc/308578/

Prakash, P. (2020, October 30). *How LLCs pay taxes*. Nerd Wallet. https://www.nerdwallet.com/article/small-business/small-business-llc-taxes#:~:text=LLC%20tax%20tips%20for%20business%20owners&text=Here%20are%20some%20tips%20for

Reuting, J. (2016a, March 26). *10 things to avoid doing with an LLC*. Dummies. https://www.dummies.com/article/business-careers-money/business/ small-business/general-small-business/10-things-to-avoid-doing-with-an-llc-149276/

Reuting, J. (2016b, March 26). *How you want your limited liability company to be managed*. Dummies. https://www.dummies.com/article/business-careers-money/business/small-business/general-small-business/how-you-want-your-limited-liability-company-to-be-managed-148505/

Reuting, J. (2016c, March 26). *Operating your limited liability company (LLC)*. Dummies. https://www.dummies.com/article/business-careers-money/ business/small-business/general-small-business/operating-your-limited-liability-company-llc-148510/

Simon, D. (n.d.). *The different types of LLCs*. Tailor Brands. https://www.tailor brands.com/llc-formation/types-of-llc

Steingold, D. M. (2013, January). *Notify creditors of a business closure to limit your liability*. Nolo. https://www.nolo.com/legal-encyclopedia/free-books/small-business-book/chapter12-8.html

Tax Foundation. (n.d.). *What is a gross receipts tax?* Tax Foundation. https:// taxfoundation.org/tax-basics/gross-receipts-tax/

Truic. (n.d.-a). *9 (VERY) Important things to do after forming an LLC* Truic. Howtostartanllc.com. https://howtostartanllc.com/after-forming-llc

Truic. (n.d.-b). *How to start an LLC. Starting your own LLC is easy*. How to Start an LLC. https://howtostartanllc.com/

Tucker, K. (n.d.). *The disadvantages of a single-member limited liability company audit*. Small Business - Chron.com. https://smallbusiness.chron.com/disad vantages-singlemember-limited-liability-company-audit-12741.html

TurboTax - Taxes, Income Tax. (2018). *What is a W-2 form? - TurboTax Tax tips & videos*. Intuit. https://turbotax.intuit.com/tax-tips/irs-tax-forms/what-is-a-w-2-form/L6VJbqWl5

U.S Small Business Administration. (2019). *Write your business plan*. U.S Small Business Administration.https://www.sba.gov/business-guide/plan-your-business/write-your-business-plan

United States Small Business Administration. (n.d.). *Basic information about operating agreements*. U.S Small Business Administration. https://www.sba. gov/blog/basic-information-about-operating-agreements

UpCounsel. (n.d.-a). *Is a single member LLC protected?* UpCounsel. https://

www.upcounsel.com/is-a-single-member-llc-protected

UpCounsel. (n.d.-b). *LLC reporting requirements: everything you need to know.* UpCounsel. https://www.upcounsel.com/llc-reporting-requirements

UpCounsel. (n.d.-c). *Single-member LLC vs multi-member LLC: what you need to know.* UpCounsel. https://www.upcounsel.com/single-member-llc-vs-multi-member-llc

UpCounsel. (2020). *LLC Structure: Everything you need to know.* UpCounsel. https://www.upcounsel.com/llc-structure

Wang, A. L. (2022a, March 30). *What is a limited liability company? LLC pros, cons.* Nerd Wallet. https://www.nerdwallet.com/article/small-business/starting-successful-llc#benefits-of-an-llc

Wang, A. L. (2022b, April 20). *Business structure: how to choose the right one.* Nerd Wallet. https://www.nerdwallet.com/article/small-business/business-structure

Watts, R. (2021, May 6). *How to set up An LLC in 7 steps.* Forbes Advisor. https://www.forbes.com/advisor/business/how-to-set-up-an-llc-in-7-steps/

Watts, R. (2022, March 25). *How to dissolve an LLC.* Forbes Advisor. https://www.forbes.com/advisor/business/how-to-dissolve-an-llc/

Wong, B. (2022, October 27). *How to open an LLC bank account.* Legal Zoom. https://www.legalzoom.com/articles/how-to-open-an-llc-bank-account

Dropdesk. (2020, August 3). 101 inspirational quotes for startups. The Remote Worker by DropDesk. https://drop-desk.com/blog/startup-quotes

Denise E (October 13, 2021). *LLC Facts.* Funds Net. https://fundsnetservices.com/llc-facts

Harris R (08 June 2020). *A new understanding of the history of limited liability: an invitation for theoretical reframing.* Cambridge Core. https://www.cambridge.org/core/journals/journal-of-institutional-economics/article/new-understanding-of-the-history-of-limited-liability-an-invitation-for-theoretical-reframing/B12B69696AC81304A2738ADE4FFF4556

Houston M (n.d). *Mastering The Basics Of Business Finance Management.* https://www.forbes.com/sites/melissahouston/2023/03/22/mastering-the-basics-of-business-finance-management/?sh=18eb27895a8f

Murray J (September 19, 2022). *LLC - Limited Liability Company Myths.* The Balance. https://www.thebalancemoney.com/limited-liability-company-myths-398639